THE RACE TO

IMMORTALITY

THE STORY OF CALIFORNIA CHROME AND HIS ATTEMPT

AT RACING HISTORY

BY MICHAEL E. KENESKI

Immortal. This simple eight-letter word originates from the Middle English language going back to the year 1300 A.D. It is defined as a "quality of enduring life" or "enduring fame." One simple word but a very deep and rich meaning. Immortal has traversed its way around the modern English language with a somewhat wide meaning. Often however it has entered into the sports lexicon across many different disciplines. Its most optimal meaning has ultimately found itself reserved for athletic greats such as Wayne Gretzky, Michael Jordan, and Tiger Woods in their respective sports. For the Muhammad Ali's, Jack Nicklaus', and Bobby Orr's. For Babe Ruth, Wilt Chamberlain, and Bobby Jones. And of course for the 11 Triple Crown winners that began in 1919 with Sir Baton and spanned all the way to 1978's Affirmed. With only 11 horses successfully completing the Triple Crown (winning the Kentucky Derby, Preakness, and Belmont Stakes) in over 100 years of racing, those who were able to conquer such a grueling stretch of three distinctly different races in the span of five weeks, all became worthy of being labeled an immortal. It was with this backdrop that a foal born on February 18th, 2011 and given the name California Chrome, began to embark on a journey that would not only capture the attention and hearts of mainstream America but in the process revive a pursuit for immortality that had done been accomplished in 36 long years. Owned by two working class men who named their one-horse organization "Dumb Ass Stables" and trained by a 73-year-old racing lifer whose last connection to a Triple Crown champion came in the 1950's, California Chrome was a story that needed to be seen to be believed. Believe we all did however. Believed that a horse could buck all the odds and push back all the naysayers who argued a Triple Crown could never be done again. Believed that gentlemen from humble beginnings and backgrounds could rise to the top of a sport often dominated by the rich and royalty. Believed that a horse sired by a complete disaster of a race horse by the name of Love The Chase, could turn out to be an awesome mix of size and speed that made the sport of racing his own. All that belief and a healthy dose of fate came together on June 7th, 2014 at approximately 6:50 PM Eastern Time when California Chrome attempted to become the 12th member of the Triple Crown club. While he would ultimately come up short, California Chrome's story was an adventure all its own.

THE BEGINNING

They loved horse racing. Two middle-aged men with a bit of extra spending money to their names, although not to the point of going crazy. Two men who dreamed quietly and eventually to one another about how cool it would be to one day own a racehorse. Maybe win a big stakes or two. Maybe make a little bit of money. And who knows if they got lucky, maybe they could stumble onto a "special" horse. One who could one day run in the Kentucky Derby. Why not us right? How many times has a story been told of an unknown owner who had a feeling about a horse that no one else did. Whose dedication and refusal to quit finally was rewarded with an invite to Louisville on the first Saturday in May. To see the Twin Spires in all their majesty. To rub shoulders with the rich and famous who annually descended on the Kentucky Derby since that "was the place to be seen."

For two men by the names of Steve Cobun from Topaz Lake, Nevada and Perry Martin from Yuba City, California, their ability to dream was just like anyone else's. So they did the only thing they thought they could do given their portfolio and tax brackets as far as getting into the horse racing industry. Not having nearly enough money to purchase a horse between the two of them, Martin and Perry soon entered into a syndicate group in order to get their foot into the racing door. A syndicate ownership is a fancy way of saying that a bunch of individuals pooled their resources together in order to gather up enough money to purchase a horse. And in this case that horse was a filly by the name of Love The Chase. Both Coburn and Martin loved her name. It had a nice racing touch to it. And since neither man knew much of anything about how to evaluate a racehorse, the aura of positive vibes they felt with Love The Chase's name was all they had to go on as they put in their money and became part of the team. Unfortunately for Martin, Perry, and the rest of the syndicate, they didn't have a female version of Funny Cide on their hands (the Derby and Preakness champ was owned by a group of childhood friends who didn't have enough money to travel as a team in anything but a yellow school bus). Instead Love The Chase was a horrendous racehorse who was extremely slow a foot and whose body proved ill-equipped for the rigors of racing. The entire syndicate outside of Martin and Perry wanted out within a short time, seeing nothing to gain and more money to lose. Martin and Perry were not going to give up easily however, especially since they continued to feel a connection to their investment. So in a move that many in the industry openly mocked, both men put up the $8,000 needed to own Love The Chase outright. The reaction to their purchase bordered on disbelief in the racing world. The mocking got to the point where a bold groomer in Love The Chase's stable was even overheard saying that anyone who would pay that kind of money for such a dud of a racehorse was a "dumbass." Despite the scathing remark, Perry and Martin

5

instead reacted by playing on the comment as the new name for their "stable" of runners, which of course was still made up entirely of Love The Chase. Thus "Dumb Ass Partners" was born as Martin and Perry used some self-depreciating humor to make the best of their on seemingly ugly ownership situation.

With both feet (and $8,000) fully into the deep end of racing with Love The Chase, Martin and Perry soon decided that their best course of action was to try and breed her with a stallion who could hopefully produce a even modestly better racer. They discovered a candidate by the name of Lucky Pulpit whose owners were asking for only a $2,000 stud fee. Both men liked the muscular form of Lucky Pulpit and so they agreed to the sum in a "what the heck" gesture.

The romance apparently blossomed between the two as soon Love The Chase was pregnant and eventually she gave birth months later. Out came a beautiful-looking colt who had a majestic appearance to him in the form of a white blaze streaking down his face and possessing four white feet. Showing his feistiness coming right out of the womb, the infant colt injured Love The Chase by kicking her uterus; spilling blood all over the stall. Luckily Love The Chase survived and her colt began to quickly grow into his physically impressive body. Martin and Perry eventually decided to give him the name California Chrome, due to the location of his birth and for the white markings on his face and feet which both owners were fascinated by. Presented with a new runner to work with, Martin and Perry decided to enlist an aging trainer by the name of Art Sherman to figure out what to do with him. California Chrome's owners liked Sherman's story as a trainer who was once forced to sleep on a pile of hay as he accompanied his 1955 Kentucky Derby contending horse by the name of Swaps as they traveled from Los Angeles to Louisville. Swaps would go on to win the Derby which meant Sherman had to know something with regards to elevating a horse to such heights. Even if the victory came over 50 years ago.

Still Sherman liked what he saw out of California Chrome after finally meeting up with him right after officially being hired. Despite his advancing age, Sherman longed for one more shot at a Derby crown. To be relevant again in the always unforgiving sport of horse racing. While no one knew what Perry and Martin had with this unknown colt, Sherman was instantly drawn to California Chrome and eagerly set out to start putting potential and physical ability together on the track. While California Chrome was still a few months away from turning 2, which would usher in the official start of his racing career, Sherman quickly put his new charge to work in order for him to literally hit the ground running when the calendar turned. No one, including Sherman, had any idea what California Chrome was or could be. However every journey needs a starting point and California Chrome was ready to write his own story. For better or for worse.

2-YEAR-OLD CAMPAIGN

With Sherman working with California Chrome on an almost daily basis early in his age-2 season, all involved eventually felt that the time had come to see what the team had at their disposal by unleashing their colt onto the racetrack in competition. California Chrome was soon entered into his first race at Hollywood Park Racetrack in April 2013. Ridden by Alberto Delgado, who was one of the more prominent jockeys on the West Coast, California Chrome came in second by only a length. All involved agreed it was not a bad debut by any means for California Chrome and he quickly was entered into his second race three weeks later, also under the guidance of Delgado. This time California Chrome crossed the wire first, giving Perry and Martin their first official victories as racehorse owners.

As they say in sports, winning is like a drug you can never get enough of. With that desire to win comes the idea of raising the stakes so that the payoff is so much sweeter. For Perry, Martin, and Art Sherman, elevating California Chrome into his first stakes race was the inevitable next step in his development. It was soon decided that they would enter California Chrome into the Willard Proctor Memorial a month later, where he would be considered one of the primary contenders in the nine-horse field. Corey Nakatani replaced Alberto Delgado on the mount due to a scheduling conflict for the latter. Nakatani's inexperience riding California Chrome showed in the race and the result also showed that maybe

Sherman had to go back to the drawing board a bit on his horse. After challenging for the lead early on, California Chrome tired and wound up finishing a lackluster fifth. For Sherman, it appeared that California Chrome was not yet ready physically to run at the intensity he needed for a stakes race, given his poor showing. As a result California Chrome was given the next six weeks off from racing as Sherman went to work on his fitness level. While California Chrome proved he had the speed to gun to the lead, his ability to pace and save something for the end push was not there yet.

Eventually all the hard work paid off as California Chrome claimed his first stakes win (and second career victory) in the Graduation Stakes at Del Mar under the ride of Alberto Delgado once again. Delgado seemed to have a rapport with California Chrome and the horse's second win in four tries began to embolden Perry and Martin that maybe sticking with Love The Chase all along didn't make them such "dumbasses." What was different this time around however was that Sherman decided to use blinkers on California Chrome, while also medicating him with Lasix. While the blinkers helped keep California Chrome focused, the Lasix helped prevent bleeding in his lungs which would boost his endurance. After the Graduation Stakes win, there were positives all around and the good vibes from California Chrome's win with Delgado back in the saddle meant that an attempt for the first time in a grades stakes beckoned.

Carefully choosing where California Chrome would undertake his first big stakes challenge, Sherman decided that the seven-furlong Grade1 Del Mart Futurity was a good match. There was a large field of 11 horses entered into the mix, with California Chrome assigned 122 pounds. Once again battling to the front of the pack, California Chrome encountered some stiff traffic trouble which Delgado was not able to steer him out of. He would finish a dull sixth out of 11.

Calling the Del Mar Futurity a "bad race" which could be blamed on the traffic, Sherman felt the Golden State Juvenile Stakes at Santa Anita two months later would be California Chrome's next attempt to get back on racing track. The November 1st race was the undercard to the Breeders' Cup which meant that California Chrome would be running in front of the biggest crowd he had ever encountered which worried Sherman a bit. California Chrome had shown himself to be a bit jittery in the starting gate and there was concern by Sherman that he drew post 1 which meant his horse would be loaded first and have to wait out everyone else. That increased the risk of California Chrome acting up in the gate, expending nervous energy, and possibly getting injured.

Sherman's concerns proved right on target as California Chrome was visibly excitable soon after being loaded on race day. The outing itself was a disaster as California Chrome finished a lackluster sixth for the second straight time. With only two wins in his first six races, the last two being sizable duds, a change was being mulled by California Chrome's connections. Specifically speaking, Sherman spoke with Perry and Martin about making a jockey change as it looked like Delgado and California Chrome had peaked as a pair. While all involved liked and respected Delgado, it was felt that the pairing had "stalled out" and a fresh approach was needed. After mulling over a replacement, Sherman remembered that he had crossed paths during his time stationed in Northern California with a rising jock by the name of Victor Espinoza who would eventually turn out to be one of the best in the sport. The call was soon made to officially make the switch and Espinoza earned the mount for California Chrome's last race of the year as a 2-year-old, the December 22nd King Glorious Stakes at Hollywood Park.

In addition to the arrival of Espinoza into the California Chrome family, Sherman also proceeded to hire Alberto Delgado's brother Willie as his exercise rider. After failing to make it as a jockey or a trainer in Maryland, Delgado moved out west to hook up with his brother, thus coming into inevitable contact with Sherman where the two soon became friendly. Loving Willie's work ethic and tenderness with horses, Sherman felt he was the best fit as the exercise rider, despite the awkwardness of having to fire his brother as California Chrome's jockey. As they say however, business is business.

　　With all the changes completed on the prep team, it was once again time to race and see if Espinoza could help unleash the potential that resided in California

Chrome. Despite the lack of attention on racing with Christmas looming, California Chrome ran the type of race in the King Glorious Stakes which generates pub for next year's Kentucky Derby. Bursting out of the gate and showing none of the drawbacks that stunted his growth earlier, California Chrome dominated the King Glorious Stakes by more than 6 lengths. Espinoza was bubbly afterwards, exclaiming to Sherman that he wanted to be "put on more of those." It was also on this day that Sherman began to seriously think he had a Triple Crown contender on his hands.

PREPPING FOR THE DERBY/3-YEAR OLD CAMPAIGN BEGINS

With Sherman giddy to get started with California Chrome and his all-important three-year-old campaign, he didn't wait long to try and engineer a follow up to his colt's shockingly great victory in last December's King Glorious Stakes. California Chrome would quickly be entered into the January 5th California Cup Derby where he would go off as the second favorite once again under the guidance of Espinoza. Despite taking some time to get up to speed out of the gate, California Chrome kicked it into high gear like he did in the King Glorious, passing horses with little effort as he headed into the homestretch. It was there that Espinoza gave a quick whip to California Chrome who all of a sudden went off like a cannon, drawing away from the rest of the field by 5 1/2 lengths. Clearly it was starting to become obvious that California Chrome was developing into a big time talent and Sherman was effusive in his praise afterwards. "I thought he would run awesome. He'd been training like a bomb."

With the California Cup Derby giving his California Chrome a two-race winning streak, Sherman began to map out the four months leading up to Louisville. Sherman concluded that California Chrome had time for two more races to give himself enough earnings to qualify for the Derby and in the process not overwork him leading up to the race. Next up on the docket would be the March 8th Grade 2 San Felipe Stakes which carried a $300,500 purse. In a field of seven, California

Chrome figured to be challenged by Midnight Hawk who was a horse who liked to engage in speed duels. At 1 1/16th of a mile, the San Felipe would test California Chrome's endurance as the Derby loomed with its mile-and-a-quarter distance.

Once the gates popped open, Sherman quickly realized that California Chrome would get the test he needed regarding his endurance to run past a mile as Midnight Hawk pressed him right away. The two quickly engaged in a speed duel that cooked the track and left the other five runners a collective non-factor. Running the half in a blistering :45, California Chrome continued to draw ahead as Midnight Hawk began to labor. With his rival now falling back, California Chrome refused to let up despite not being whipped by Espinoza. He would go on to take the San Felipe in a torrid 1:09 2/3's for his third victory in a row.

What really caught Sherman's eye in the San Felipe was the ease at which he ran the 1 1/6th of a mile and how California Chrome also burst out of the gate in the same manner he did in his previous two races. The patterns were starting to fit. "I wanted to try something new today so I let him go right out of the gate," Espinoza said. "I don't know if people expected me to go right to the lead but I wanted to let him enjoy his race, I just let him go. It seems like he likes both tracks. He's been training over at Los Al but he does things so much easier at Santa Anita after having trained at Los Al. He didn't feel tired at all after the wire." Sherman himself found it tough not to start boasting about California Chrome's abilities, in particular his belief that distance was not a problem.

"I didn't think he'd be on the lead, but he was a handful today," said Sherman. "I just told Victor, 'You got him.' I told him he broke like that because of that Quarter Horse training at Los Alamitos … We all know Santa Anita's a speed-biased type of track, so it was really great to see him with the hold he had on him. It's unbelievable. I don't think the distance will make any difference, a mile and a quarter," said Sherman in reference to the Kentucky Derby distance. "I think he'll run all day."

The buzz was beginning to percolate regarding California Chrome and his sudden domination on the West Coast. With his latest victory, California Chrome had increased his earnings well into the upper tier of the three-year-old crop which meant he was a virtual lock for the Derby. However there was one more race to go, the all-important Derby prep which would once and for all place California Chrome into a certain category of contender for Louisville. With the Wood Memorial, Florida Derby, and Illinois Derby all options, Sherman would elect to stay on the West Coast for the Santa Anita on April 8th.

THE SANTA ANITA DERBY

Despite California Chrome coming into the Santa Anita Derby on a four-race winning streak, Art Sherman, Steve Coburn, and Perry Martin were filled with nerves. With their virtually automatic inclusion to the Derby at hand, all California Chrome had to do was come through the race without incident in order for his owners to realize their dreams of owning a horse that would compete the first Saturday in May. Not to mention Sherman being given the chance to come full circle in going back to the Derby as a trainer 53 years later. The magnitude of the moment was made even greater when Perry and Martin were offered $6 million for a 51% controlling interest in California Chrome prior to the race. In addition if they agreed to do the deal, the duo would have to fire Sherman and install a different trainer. Clearly Perry and Martin were no longer being seen as "dumb" in the racing community and the $6 million offer was validation that they had a special horse on their hands. The offer was subsequently rejected as Martin and Perry went with the "we have come this far" mantra as they settled in to watch California Chrome in the 1 1/8th mile prep.

As the favorite among eight entered, California Chrome had quite a bit of pressure to perform in such a big race with the Derby just a few weeks away. With potent challengers such as the highly regarded Hoppertunity and Candy Boy in the field, California Chrome would have to earn his most important potential victory to

16

date. After an incident-free loading, the gates sprung open with California Chrome immediately encountering his first challenge of the day. Having a bit of a poor reaction time to the start, California Chrome failed to jump out to the lead like he had been doing the last few races. Instead he became wedged between the field which interrupted his stride a bit early on. However in choosing to remain calm despite the early setback, Espinoza guided California Chrome out from the inside and found a stalking lane by the quarter pole. It was there that he made his move, drawing out into the lead and opening up daylight as he entered into the stretch. The rest of the field could only watch as California Chrome once again busted clear of the pack, running with a powerful glide that allowed Espinoza to actually ease up as they approached the finish. California Chrome would go on to win by 5 1/2 lengths, with Hoppertunity finishing second, followed by Candy Boy in third.

The Santa Anita result was staggeringly brilliant for California Chrome as he registered a 107 Beyer speed figure, which would turn out to be the number one mark of any participant in any of the prep races that day. Once again California Chrome showed that he was for real and was now possibly going to go into the Derby as the betting favorite after upping his winning streak to five. The result also allowed Sherman the chance to wax poetic about just how good California Chrome was. "He's my Swaps," said Sherman. "I can't believe the races I've been seeing. A length or two would have been all right by me. I might have to go back to riding if this keeps up, what do you think? Look at him. Look at when he stretches out. This is what I love about him. Oh my goodness! How many lengths to you think? Eight maybe? When I saw him opening up, I said to myself, 'wow." That was the only thing I could say…. He's been training like a bomb the last three weeks. My expectations were high, but this exceeded them."

Espinoza was equally effusive in his excitement for California Chrome, exclaiming "the most important thing to me was to have a clean run when I hit the first turn." After that, it was easy for me…. Right now he's on his game and has a lot of confidence. He has this unbelievable heart and he just wants to run." Asked to compare his Triple Crown close call on War Emblem, Espinoza answered "The only thing is they're a different color."

Clearly the hype machine was in overdrive for California Chrome as he looked ahead to the Kentucky Derby. In fact installed as the betting favorite, California Chrome would now have all the world watching as he attempted to become the rare top choice to claim the roses. The momentum had built to a crescendo when it came to California Chrome's Derby prep and there was no stopping him now according to Sherman, Espinoza, Martin, and Perry. The dream would be fulfilled by all just in showing up to the Derby with an entrant. Now there was an opportunity at hand to make that dream a reality.

THE DERBY DRAW

As expected, a full field of 20 horses was entered to make the Kentucky Derby the equine equivalent of parkway traffic at 5:00 PM. With so many horses bunched together in a mad dash around the 1 1/4-mile Churchill Downs track, often the Kentucky Derby has been called a race where the winner has the most "luck" in trying to find open lanes in such a big field. Be that as it may, all 20 entrants and their connections possessed vivid dreams of winning the Derby, wearing the roses, and beginning a possible quest for the Triple Crown. The Wednesday before the race was the all-important post position draw, yet another crucial exercise that could help or severely inhibit a given horse's chances in the Derby. Drawing post 1 or 2 right near the rail is especially dreaded due to the likelihood of being boxed in by the rest of the field. In addition drawing the extreme outside posts is also quite undesirable due to every jockey's stated attempts to save as much ground for their horse as possible, thus saving energy for a late run. Having to start out so wide leaves the jockey with an unenviable decision about whether to gun to the lead in order to move in near the rail (using up precious energy right out of the gate) or instead sitting back while moving inside as the front-runners take off. That scenario puts the jockey and horse in the position of hoping for a fast pace so that those near the lead tire themselves out which makes a late charge possible.

In the end, somewhere in the middle is generally agreed to be the best path to possible victory, as there are many more options on the table as the race unfolds. With all that said, Art Sherman acted incredibly evasive leading into the draw about where he liked to have seen California Chrome end up. Minutes later Sherman would draw the fifth post, a spot that he didn't seem particularly pleased about based on body language and his less than enthusiastic answer on his thoughts afterwards. "That's fine. If he breaks well, he's got enough speed to stay out of trouble." Meanwhile Victor Espinoza raised a few eyebrows when he noted that Derby-Preakness winner War Emblem drew the fifth spot before he won in Louisville. Either way California Chrome was installed as the 5-2 morning-line favorite, with Hoppertunity the second choice at 6-1, and Wicked Strong completing the top three at 8-1. With California Chrome possibly making Sherman the oldest trainer to win the Derby in racing history, the increasing magnitude of the moment didn't seem to be rattling him outwardly. "I'm happy and feel no pressure. I'm going to relax the next couple days and enjoy some of the parties." California Chrome at the same time was sitting idly in his stall, with nary a care in the world as the Derby favorite.

THE KENTUCKY DERBY

Derby Day. Just that statement along is enough to get the chills rolling and the excitement heightened as the first Saturday in May arrives. The level of extravagance for the Derby is unmatched by quite possible any other major sporting event as big time actors, actresses, sports celebrities, and titans of the business world arrive in Louisville en masse for the pre-race parties, the scene itself, or really just to enjoy some top end racing. While 99.9 percent of the second-biggest crowd in Derby history (163,906) were enjoying a day where their biggest concern was how to keep their mint juleps cold, the owners and trainers of the 20 horses in the main event were a ball of nerves. In particular, Perry Martin would quickly be overwhelmed by the sheer size of the crowd, retreating to the clubhouse in order to try and prevent a full-blown panic attack. Steve Coburn meanwhile tried to stay close to the action, mingling with anyone who wanted to get close to him as he heard more than a few "you look like Wilfred Brimley" comments. Finally, Art Sherman kept a low profile himself, so as not to have to answer more questions about possibly becoming the oldest trainer of a Derby winner.

On a day full of early spring sunshine as the large undercard moved through one race after the other, the moment would finally be at hand as the call for "Rider's Up!" echoed around the track. As the jockeys began to mount their rides,

California Chrome was the picture of calm as he moved his head back and forth in reaction to the deafening crowd that got louder with each stride that brought the field to the starting gate.

When it comes to a field the magnitude of the 20-horse Derby field, loading staff on the track make it a point to enter in the horses two at a time so as to cut down on the idle time where incidents of agitation could quickly occur. On this day however, everyone was on their best behavior as all 2o horses were quickly locked and loaded, awaiting the start for the 'Run For The Roses.'

As the gates flung open, signaling the start of the 140th Kentucky Derby, California Chrome broke out with a slight wobble that didn't inhibit his stride noticeably. Espinoza quickly charged to the front of the pack in order to follow through on Art Sherman's idea of not allowing themselves to get caught in the middle of the huge pack. Once Espinoza got California Chrome to a stalking position in third, he eased up a bit as pacesetters Uncle Sigh (30-1) and Chitu (25-1) led the procession around the first turn and into the start of the backstretch. Watching the clock with nervous anticipation was Sherman, knowing that a fast or even brisk pace could be trouble with regards to California Chrome being able to have enough energy to finish.

As they headed for the all-important half-mile split, Uncle Sigh and Chitu continued to sit on top as California Chrome bided his time in a comfortable stride.

They would pass the half-mile mark in a very slow 47.1 which was a very telling number on a few different fronts. For one, the slow pace meant that a closer was not going to win the Derby on this day. With the front of the pack horses not having to run overly hard to that point, there would be energy in reserve remaining for more than a few which included California Chrome. Sherman had to be ecstatic over the time, realizing that California Chrome would be in an almost perfect spot to strike once the overmatched Uncle Sigh and Chitu backed up.

The far turn soon approached as Uncle Sigh and Chitu started to fall back as the distance began to get the better of their limited pedigrees. California Chrome meanwhile began to make his move, pulling up next to those two while being joined closely to an also advancing Samraat. In addition the highly regarded Danza put himself right to the front as well which had to be concerning to Sherman since he was mentioned prominently by himself and many in the racing community as a prime contender to win. That worry would quickly dissipate as California Chrome moved into first place at the start of the stretch and than began to make his determined charge ahead. Samraat was the only horse even somewhat close to California Chrome at that point but the gap between the two quickly grew to as many as five lengths. As the lead continued to grow, it was now a foregone conclusion that California Chrome would win the Derby, which he made a formality a few strides later. So dominant was California Chrome down the stretch that Espinoza was able to ease up on his ride as Commanding Curve ran all-out to take second, joined closely behind by Danza for third. The rest of the field mattered little however as this was California Chrome's day in becoming the rare betting favorite to claim the roses in a time of 2:03.66 which would be the slowest winning Derby mark since 1972 on a fast track.

Bedlam ensued all around Sherman and Coburn, with tears in the eyes of both. Martin meanwhile stayed secluded, so overwhelming the whole day had been for him. Leading up to the race much was made about the incredible confidence Coburn had in California Chrome, going so far as to guaranteeing his victory. Still on this day Coburn credited other sources for his colt's run. "Our guardian angels have been watching over us and they put our horse on the right path." Coburn and Sherman were quickly joined by Espinoza, who had just won his second Derby which placed him on an elevated level among the always-competitive jockey community. "Everything worked out. An amazing race, this horse has so much talent. By the three-eighths pole, he was going so strong, and I could see the other horses struggling a bit. I let him go, and that was it." Sherman meanwhile allowed himself to flashback to his days as a jockey watching California Chrome rampage down the stretch. "When he spurted away, I said, 'Let me take over for the last 70 yards,' and I rode him in with Victor."

Overall the Derby win was worth $1,417,800 which increased California Chrome's

career earnings to 2,752,650. Sherman also officially claimed the title of oldest

trainer to ever win the Derby at 77-years-old, which passed Charlie Whittingham

who was 76 when he accomplished the trick in 1989. Putting everything into clear

perspective on this very emotional day, Sherman admitted his true thoughts right

before the race. "I said a little prayer," he said, "and it came true. Now California

Chrome is my Swaps." Asked if life would be different now that he was a

champion again, Sherman wouldn't take the bait. "I'm still the same Art Sherman,"

he said, "except I've won the Kentucky Derby."

As the euphoria of winning the Derby circled all around, Sherman also

began to realize something else through all of the cheering and pats on the back.

Taking home the roses was only the start. The Preakness was a short two weeks

away and so it was almost already time to get back to work in order to see if this

whole Triple Crown thing was even possible. For one day however, Sherman

would allow himself to bask in the glory. In possibly getting caught up in the

moment for a nanosecond, Sherman blurted out at the end of his press conference

for all the world to hear

"He's the rock star, and I'm just the manager," Sherman said. "And we're

going all the way."

One down and two to go. The path to immortality had really just begun.

STILL BASKING IN THE DERBY GLOW WHILE LOOKING AHEAD TO PIMLICO

Perry Martin, Steve Coburn, and indirectly even Art Sherman got the last laugh. After it was widely reported that Martin and Coburn rejected a $6 million offer for a 51 percent stake in California Chrome prior to the Derby (an offer that if agreed upon would have cost Sherman his job), it would have been easy for ownership to tell the whole world how smart they were to hold pat with their colt. However in true understated fashion, Martin and Perry refused to boast and instead reveled in all the work they had put in to get to the Louisville winner's circle on the first Saturday in May.

"To see this all happen for me and my partner and our wives, to see this dream come true, means so much," Coburn said not even 24 hours after California Chrome took home the roses. "We have put so much blood, sweat and tears, our savings, our retirement, into this horse." Sherman meanwhile was now fully focusing in on the upcoming Preakness which at a mile-and-3/16 was a bit shorter than the Derby in distance. Still Sherman voiced concern about the two-week turnaround at another locale with a bunch of fresh shooters ready to take their shot at the soon-to-be overwhelming favorite. "To be honest, I'm not too comfortable with running him back in two weeks but I know that's what we're bound to do. I'm the kind of guy who likes to wait seven or eight weeks between races. These horses run hard and they need time to recover."

With regards to possible challengers for the Preakness, only Ride on Curlin and General A Rod vowed to join California Chrome in running the first two legs of the series. Meanwhile the highly touted Social Inclusion, trained by the legendary Bob Baffert, was lying in wait to destroy the Triple Crown dreams of his counterpart. Having suffered heartbreak on three different occasions on the doorstep to greatness, Baffert was now in position to return the favor.

PREAKNESS POST DRAW

As he had planned it out right after the Derby, Art Sherman went back to his Los Alamitos stable for a few days while son Alan accompanied California Chrome on the long van ride east to the decaying Pimlico racetrack. Unlike pristine Churchill Downs, the Pimlico track had seen better days. From paint that was peeling off some of the walls, to a grandstand that needed an update about ten years earlier, Pimlico had become a shell of its former glamorous self. It even had gotten to the point in the last few years where talk began about possibly moving the Preakness to a more upscale track, so disturbing was its visual decline. Aesthetics aside, the race still had to be run where of course California Chrome would try to repel the challenges from 9 other colts, only two of whom went down in defeat at Louisville.

The post draw for the Preakness can considered somewhat of a yawnfest given the much lower importance of positioning in the less crowded field. Past winners have come from almost every spot along the starting gate so there was not a whole lot of urgency for Art Sherman regarding where California Chrome would take off from. Joining Sherman at the post draw was Coburn who took the opportunity to add another chapter to his growing "Nostradamus of Nevada" persona. "I knew this horse was going to win the Kentucky Derby," Coburn said shortly before the draw. "Honestly think he'll win the Preakness, too. The big test will be the Belmont." Shortly after Coburn spoke, California Chrome drew the number 3 post and was installed as the 3-5 favorite. Baffert's Social Inclusion meanwhile drew the 5 post and would be the second favorite at 5-1. Fellow new shooter Bayern joined returnee Ride On Curlin to round out the top betting favorites by both going off at 10-1.

Sherman himself seemed unbothered about the post position when he met with reporters shortly afterward. "The 3 is fine," he said. "Most of the speed is outside of us, and if they go, we can track in behind them. My horse likes a target to run at. If Victor [Espinoza] looks outside and sees that nobody is going, we can take the lead. I just keep my fingers crossed we have a good trip. I wouldn't want to be in anybody else's shoes right now." He went on to point out that California Chrome had actually put on weight since his Kentucky Derby victory which went in stark contrast to the trend of Louisville winners dropping some pound heading into Baltimore due to all the work they put in leading up to the races. "It always bothers me coming back in two weeks," he said. "I know it's a tradition, but it's hard on the horses. But he's eating good and seems to be thriving, so let's go for it."

All system were a go for California Chrome with the Preakness just days away. Cross the wire first and a date with greatness would be set for three weeks at the unforgiving Belmont Stakes. Go down in defeat and California Chrome becomes just another name that would eventually be forgotten like Fusaichi

Pegasus, Super Saver, Animal Kingdom, and Monarchos who all won the Derby, only to see their Triple Crown dreams go up in smoke 14 days later at the Preakness. As always fate would play a role in how everything would ultimately play out but at the very least California Chrome appeared to be clicking on all cylinders, right on down to the confidence of his trainer and owners.

THE PREAKNESS STAKES

With only nine challengers set to try and deny California Chrome his shot at a possible Triple Crown, the road to the wire would naturally be less chaotic and traffic-dependent with regards to the possible winner. In addition, outside of only Social Inclusion and Ride on Curlin, no one with even a passing knowledge of thoroughbred racing gave any other horse a chance to get under the wire ahead of California Chrome. However with the Pimlico turns being much tighter than the ones at Churchill Downs, Victor Espinoza laid out a plan early on race day with Sherman regarding the idea of gunning to the front in order to control the pace and stay on top of any attempts to box in California Chrome along the rail coming out of the 3 post.

Having endured another long wait leading up to the race, Art Sherman soon made his way down to the grandstand with Steve Coburn just like they did two weeks earlier in Louisville as the Preakness field made their way to the starting gate. After suffering anxiety from the big crowd at Churchill Downs, Perry Martin decided not to attend the race which left Coburn as the face of ownership for the NBC cameras. Once again focusing in on California Chrome as he was entered into the starting gate for any signs of nervousness, Sherman had to be pleased about the tranquility of his colt as he sat patiently in post 3 while the rest of the field got loaded. Seconds later the gates swung open and the 139th Preakness was officially underway.

As far as the start was concerned, California Chrome broke exceptionally as noted by race announcer Larry Collmus. Quickly moving to the front of the pack, California Chrome would be joined by front-runners Pablo Del Monte and filly Ria Antonia. Espinoza moved California Chrome to the outside of both as they began to race around the first turn. Meanwhile Bob Baffert had to be disappointed about the fact Social Inclusion, another colt who likes to gun to the lead, instead had to settle back in fourth place behind the leaders. As they moved along the backstretch, Pablo Del Monte continued to set the pace with Rio Antonio underneath Calvin Borel rating just behind in second. Collmus again made it a point to praise California Chrome, noting how he was in excellent position with his stalking third position. With Pablo Del Monte running the half in a pedestrian 46.4, California Chrome was being presented with the exact pace scenario from the Derby which would allow him to save energy for the push home.

As the field approached the far turn, Ria Antonia began to wilt badly as the distance swallowed the overmatched filly. It was here where both California Chrome and the charging Social Inclusion made their move along the outside of the still-leading Pablo Del Monte. The anticipated duel between Social Inclusion and California Chrome was now looking like it would unfold as many predicted.

32

However the problem for Social Inclusion was that his charge came three-wide as California Chrome saved some more ground on the inside of his foe. Still both would quickly pass the tiring Pablo Del Monte and enter the top of the stretch almost side-by-side.

Once through the far turn and now steadying for home, California Chrome began to open up a bit on Social Inclusion who bucked to the right after taking a wide turn into the top of the stretch. The additional movement seemed to immediately disrupt the stride of Social Inclusion who began to fall behind by an increasing margin. Still California Chrome was not home free yet as an outside threat began to materialize in the form of his vanquished Derby opponent Ride On Curlin. With 300 yards to go Ride On Curlin began to slightly bite into California Chrome's lead as the deafening crowed urged their new hero on. At 200 yards Ride on Curlin moved even closer as it looked like for a moment California Chrome was finally showing the first signs of fatigue. However there would be no upset on this day as California Chrome pushed out one last burst of energy that opened up some more daylight between the two and ultimately allowed him to coast past the wire for the win. Ride on Curlin would finish second by a length, General A Rod third, and Social Inclusion a fading fourth. Espinoza meanwhile pumped his first in excitement while Coburn sat down in his seat in a near-sobbing state of emotion. Sherman meanwhile was not even sure California Chrome had won due to the fact his 5-2 frame had trouble seeing over the throng surrounding him who were jumping up and down in excitement. "Everyone was cheering and jumping up and down in front of me. But when I looked up at the board and saw him moving away, I knew we were OK. I have a tear in my eye. It's a dream for any trainer to do this, believe me."

After dismounting California Chrome in the winner's circle, Espinoza was still full of jubilation after completing the Derby-Preakness double for the second time in his career. Noting how much harder his colt had to run this time around, Espinoza admitted he had to push California Chrome earlier than he had anticipated. "I had to go then, not hard, but sooner than in the Derby. That's hard on a horse, but he proved he could do it, and we got to the wire first. It's an amazing feeling to have a horse like him."

The Preakness win by California Chrome brought his victory streak to six. He also increased his career earnings to $3,452,650 after taking the $900,000 first prize in a time of 1:54.84 which was the fastest time since Big Brown in 2008. Putting the finishing touches on the day, Coburn seemed to say it all when he noted "I don't want to sound bold or cocky or arrogant but when I saw him when he was a day old, I told my wife that this colt is going to do something big, and he's never proved me wrong." Now a full 2/3rd's of the way to the Triple Crown finish line,

California Chrome was a national blockbuster story that had three weeks of hype still to go before the Belmont.

Could California Chrome do it? Could he finally end the 36-year streak of failed Triple Crown bids or was more heartache in store? For a public tired of seeing contenders come up just short in the Belmont Stakes, this one seemed a bit different. Maybe it was the fact California Chrome and his connections were easy to root for unlike what went on with Big Brown and I'll Have Another. Whatever it was, the horse racing world was bracing for another try at immortality. With only a grueling one-and-a-half mile to go, California Chrome just maybe was the one to get there.

LET THE HYPE BEGIN, CALIFORNIA CHROME ARRIVES IN NEW YORK (Tuesday May 18)

Despite the Belmont Stakes still being almost three weeks away, the connections of California Chrome wasted no time getting their Triple Crown hopeful to Elmont, Long Island in order to get an early lay of the land at Belmont Park. Accompanied during the six-hour van ride from Baltimore to New York with Preakness runner-up Ride On Curlin (clearly the two horses put aside their Triple Crown rivalry in order to keep one another company for the journey), California Chrome exited the vehicle at 10:48 ET to a round of applause from some of the Belmont Park working staff and early arrivals for the day's race card. After a quick tour of his new surroundings, California Chrome took up residence in his new home for the next two-plus weeks in stall 7 of Barn 26 which was the customary locale for any Triple Crown contender. With Art Sherman still back at his home stable in Los Alamitos, California tending to some of the other's horses in his stable, he enlisted son Alan to see California Chrome through his first few days in New York.

Meeting with the press soon after California Chrome's arrival, Alan Sherman said he planned to jog his horse that morning with exercise rider Willie Delgado and than start daily exercises beginning on Thursday. As far as any timed works were concerned, Sherman claimed that California Chrome would run only one such sprint about a week before the race. So with the itinerary laid out, Sherman began to get peppered with questions about how California Chrome was handling his new fame. "He's very inquisitive and he likes the attention. He traveled really well. He ate the whole way. And he hasn't coughed since last Tuesday." Sherman made it a point to talk about the lack of coughing from Chrome in order to put the issue to rest after all the attention it got going into the Preakness which proved to be a non-story based on the result. With that topic pushed out of the way for the time being, Sherman tried to steer the conversation back to the track and the task at hand. In answering the first of what was sure to be countless "can he do it?" questions after arriving at Belmont, Sherman revealed his prime concern regarding California Chrome's chances by saying "I just hope he handles the track. You never know until they run on it." Next Sherman thwarted a query about whether or not Chrome could handle the mile-and-a-half distance by shooting back "He's never done it but none of the others have." All true except the others horses who figured to be in the field didn't have the burden of expectations that California Chrome had.

Eventually the conversation steered to the magnitude of what was about to come and Sherman admitted to the enormity of the upcoming race and how he understood the significance of what they were about to attempt. "It means the world to all of us. It's a once-in-a-lifetime opportunity, and it's been so much fun.

I'm just so proud of my dad to be able to do this near the end of his career. He's very deserving." With feet firmly planted on the ground unlike some other boisterous trainers that came before him such as Bob Baffert and Rick Dutrow, Sherman summed everything up before getting California Chrome back to his stall by concluding that the time was right for another Triple Crown racehorse. "I think the industry could use a Triple Crown winner, especially with the story this horse has. It gives the little guy hope, and the chance something like this can happen is what makes racetrack people get up in the morning."

There were less than three weeks of mornings left for Alan and Art Sherman, Delgado, and California Chrome to get through before the moment of truth. Some more morning for something to possibly go wrong. For the cough to return. For a pin to be stepped on. For a training accident. For a denial of the precious Triple Crown. As Sherman noted it was a "one day at a time situation", with the hype growing every step of the way.

VICTOR ESPINOZA: HISTORY REPEATS ITSELF

It had been 26 years since Affirmed completed the Triple Crown with his third straight victory over famed rival Alydar, when a moody front-running speed demon by the name of War Emblem found himself just a mile-and-a-half away from joining the immortal club. On that early June day as trainer Bob Baffert watched anxiously from the grandstand in thinking maybe this could be the one after heart-wrenching denials at the wire with Real Quiet and Silver Charm years earlier, War Emblem settled into the starting gate with veteran jockey Victor Espinoza in the saddle. Just a mile-and-a half away from glory. However as it often does in horse racing, fate and the racing gods had other ideas. A split second after the gates opened up to start the procession around "Big Sandy," War Emblem stumbled forward when undertaking his first strides. With his nose almost touching dirt and Espinoza almost flying forward off his mount, War Emblem struggled to regain his footing as he soon was bumped by Medaglia D'oro to make the situation even more dire. With his stride now severely compromised and his colt stressed seconds into the race, Espinoza and War Emblem were finished before it really even got started. He would go on to finish eighth which turned out to be the worst showing ever for a Triple Crown challenger in the Belmont Stakes up to that point (Big Brown would fail to finish the race a few years later). At a loss for words when meeting with the media an hour later, Espinoza could only sum up the day tersely when he exclaimed "hey that's racing."

For Espinoza, War Emblem's flop was clearly an opportunity lost and the disappointment would stay with him years later. After cementing his status as one of the most-sought after and winning jockeys in the sport from 2000-2007 (averaging 207 victories and $12.5 million in purses), Espinoza saw his numbers slide badly as he "lost his hunger for racing." Espinoza admitted that he "got lazy and I didn't have the drive I once did" which he felt was the main reason for his decline. As a result at 37-years-old Espinoza began to seriously consider retirement. However he would admit that things changed when the longtime bachelor got serious with a woman he began dating in 2010. "I met this girl who didn't know anything about racing but after awhile she found out I'd won the Derby and asked why I hadn't won another one. She said 'Have you ever thought about doing it again?' Finally one day I woke up and said 'OK, I'll try to do it just because of you. She really motivated me. Otherwise I might be home sleeping."

Thus with fresh drive and determination to get back to the top of the racing world, Espinoza once again dove back in with both feet at the lucrative Southern California racetracks. Eventually fate and a past connection to a certain trainer by the name of Art Sherman intervened to thrust Espinoza back into the racing spotlight in a way he never could have imagined after coming so close with War

Emblem. In going back to his days as an 19-year-old apprentice at Golden Gate Fields in Northern California, Espinoza at times teamed with up Sherman who was just getting his own feet wet in the world of horse training. "I've known Victor a long time," said Sherman. "He rode a lot of winners for me in Northern California. I knew he had a lot of talent. We needed to make a change and I said I got the perfect jockey. He fits him (California Chrome) like a glove. It means a lot, the rapport between rider and horse." The two stayed in touch off and on over the years, culminating in Sherman taping Espinoza to take over for Alberto Delgado on a talented but unrefined California Chrome who had only a mediocre 2-for-6 record as a two-year-old. The rest as they say is history; or potential history as one would say. Knowing full well his good fortune for getting a precious second chance at a Triple Crown, Espinoza gushed about his good luck soon after California Chrome's victory in the Derby and Preakness. "In a million years I never thought I would get a second chance. I think the first time, some things I was not ready for." Since their pairing, Espinoza has ridden California Chrome to six wins in six races, as another bout with greatness beckoned. "California Chrome is very kind. He let's me do whatever I want to do with him. War Emblem only liked to run in front and that was very hard for me. California Chrome has tremendous talent to be able to stop and start in a race. I've never been on a horse like this. He's push-button and can open up two or three lengths in no time. When I was a kid I

41

never even thought I'd be a jockey. I never in my life dreamed of winning the Triple Crown."

Like with the rest of the connections to California Chrome, all involved took their own meandering paths to June 7th, 2014. All encountered stumbling blocks and setbacks along the way but they all also rallied to place each other into the path of potential greatness. For Victor Espinoza, the term "full circle" applied given the heartbreak he felt after War Emblem's stumble out of the gate back in 2008 with a chance for the Triple Crown and for his own career decline soon thereafter due to a lack of desire. However Espinoza's past run-ins with Art Sherman, his ability to collect winners, and his encounter with a certain lady friend all conspired to give the jockey the second chance that many before him never even had one chance at.

GETTING ACCLIMATED WITH BIG SANDY (WEDNESDAY MAY 21)

After a night spent in deep and restful sleep in stall 7 of Barn 26, the honeymoon phase was now over for California Chrome. Roused shortly after 6:00 AM by Willie Delgado, California Chrome stepped out at approximately 6:45 for his first extensive test of "Big Sandy" which was the given nickname for the main track at Belmont Park. Under the guidance of Delgado in the saddle, California Chrome jogged in a clockwise direction around the main track for 12 minutes, mixing in a brisk jog followed by a slow walk. With the outing serving as the first workout since California Chrome's Preakness victory, it was a somewhat stressful 12 minutes for Alan Sherman as the assistant trainer watched closely for any sign of trouble physically. Fortunately for Sherman and all involved, nothing untoward was found. "He actually surprised me how good he was feeling this morning. He was dragging Willie and me around the barn. It's amazing how quickly he's bouncing back off these big races he's running." Sherman reiterated that California Chrome would resume daily 6:45 AM workouts and didn't budge off his plan to have him engage in only one timed sprint. "He seemed to get over the track fine. He only jogged, so we'll learn more in the next few days galloping but he seemed fine."

As far as Delgado was concerned, the newest media darling (his effervescent smile was noted by more than a few of the new reporters in town) admitted that

California Chrome was a tad overly excited about his first job over Big Sandy. "New surroundings, he gets hyped up and tensed up. It will take him a few days to relax." Delgado did reiterate however that California Chrome was a once-in-a-lifetime horse. "After each race he's gotten stronger. It's crazy because I have never seen a horse like that."

Meanwhile later in the day California Chrome's chances of winning the Belmont Stakes and the Triple Crown got a bit better as it was revealed that prime potential spoiler Danza would not make the race after trainer Todd Pletcher failed to be impressed with his latest workout. After finishing a promising third in the Kentucky Derby and widely considered one of the best among the 3-year-old crop, Pletcher decided to scratch his colt due to Danza possibly " being tired from the spring campaign. I just sensed he wasn't 100 percent after that breeze (Danza had jogged around the Belmont track after California Chrome that morning). He's lost a little weight, has a little skin disease. Nothing major, just a little R and R should fix it." While no one from the California Chrome camp would admit it, Danza's loss could only help his chances to win the Triple Crown. Despite the loss of his star, Pletcher still planned on running both Intense Holiday (12th in the Derby) and new shooter Commissioner who placed second in the Peter Pan Stakes. Meanwhile there was 'jockeying' among the jockeys for the available mounts with still two-and-a-half weeks to go before the race.

JUST ANOTHER DAY AT THE TRACK (THURSDAY MAY 22)

True to the schedule laid out prior to the team's arrival in Elmont, California Chrome and Willie Delgado strolled out onto the main track at around 6:15 AM with only a few media members present at such an early hour. With rain having fallen off and on both in the morning and during the previous 24 hours, Delgado and Alan Sherman saw the poor weather as an opportunity to get California Chrome the chance to see what an off track from Big Sandy would feel like. Jogging near the outside fence for about a mile-and-a-half, Delgado once again gushed over his ride despite the slop. "He skipped over this track", was his quick and to he point summation over the workout.

After California Chrome's work was done for the day, Sherman once again met with the media which was noticeably smaller than the day before possibly due to the mist and rain that had kept falling. With regards to why he sent Chrome out earlier than scheduled, Sherman admitted that he "wanted to get out there before the track got chewed up. Nobody wants to train over a track like that. It was kind of sloppy but it was fine." As far as California Chrome was concerned, it was brought to Sherman's attention about how he seemed to be reveling in the attention from all the assembled cameras right along the same lines as Affirmed notably did back in 1978. "He's always liked to pose, now more than before. He's such a ham that whenever he hears a camera he stops and stares" claimed Delgado.

The growing scale of what was ahead also seemed to not bother Sherman noticeably as he remained in charge while his father continued overseeing the rest of their stable in Los Alamitos. When asked about the size of Belmont Park and what it would be like in slightly more than two weeks, Sherman admitted that the place was "massive. Your horse looks like an ant out there. This place is huge but we can handle it. This horse seems to have a lot left in the tank." While no one expected Sherman to say anything different, there was also no sign of outward bombast that would turn off the media and public like Rick Dutrow did with Big Brown. In addition, the label of "America's Horse" began to make its way around the nation, as the California Chrome hype grew with each terrific workout.

WILLIE DELGADO

The life of an exercise rider is oftentimes a thankless one. While the trainers and owners get the spotlight and 99 percent of the applause in the victory circle, the exercise rider works in relative anonymity despite spending more time on the horse than anyone else. In the case of California Chrome however, Art Sherman, Perry Martin, and Steve Coburn all seemed to make it a point to publicly praise their champion horse's exercise rider Willie Delgado who had been with the colt every step of the way towards prominence. Delgado was not unlike any other exercise rider in thoroughbred racing. Getting up at the crack of dawn to take his charges out for a stroll with no one but the chirping birds keeping him company . Getting caked with mud and dirt on the often moist early-morning tracks becomes part of the daily routine as well. Despite the monotony of the job, the exercise rider holds a significant position in the development of a racehorse as any trainer would attest. Often considered the eyes and ears of the operation due to how much time they spend on the horse, the exercise rider is instrumental in any type of racing success despite their secluded work.

While the adjustment to being an overnight celebrity can be a daunting one, as anyone associated with California Chrome became after his Derby victory, Delgado quickly showed his aptitude for witty engagements with the media during his daily chats regarding the upcoming Belmont Stakes and the possibility of his ride becoming a champion. "I'm so grateful I got this horse," Delgado gushed after another early workout around the main track. "I thank the trainer and owners every day for letting me be part of this amazing dream. A lot of people have been on the track a lot longer than I have and never got this opportunity." One only had to look at Delgado's brother Alberto who accumulated 2,823 wins in his career as a jockey. With Alberto riding in Southern California, Willie spoke about not getting many opportunities to see him given their different locales. That is until Willie visited Alberto during the summer of 2013. Willie loved the location so much that be picked up right away and moved to the West Coast to be closer to his brother. It was there that Alberto informed Willie about an impressive young 2-year-old colt he came across by the name of California Chrome. Ironically Alberto rode California Chrome to two victories during his two-year-old campaign. It was during Alberto's run as California Chrome's jockey that the exercise rider in charge at the time took a vacation. During his absence, Alberto suggested to Art Sherman that his brother was an accomplished exercise rider and that he would be perfect as a fill-in. Willie never looked back from that point forward as he took over on a full-time basis in that capacity for California Chrome. "I got lucky" Delgado would point out numerous times.

Unfortunately the family party centering on California Chrome didn't last after Alberto rode him to two straight lackluster sixth-place finishes in the middle of his two-year-old campaign. It was than that Sherman replaced Alberto with Victor Espinoza, with the rest as they say being history. Willie Delgado understood the rough side of the business however despite the sting of no longer working directly with his brother. "That's horse racing," he would say a few days after arriving at Belmont. "Albert came up to me after the Preakness and said 'You're doing a good job little brother.' At least one of us was able to get here. If we can win the Triple Crown, he'll enjoy it with me."

The big word in Willie's summation of the situation was the word "If." "If" California Chrome could buck history and become the 12th horse ever to win the Triple Crown. There would be no guarantees coming out of Delgado's mouth, at least not yet. Still too much work to do and still the threat of something going wrong. Yet another day had gone by, bringing destiny for all those involved with California Chrome another step closer. The limelight had already introduced the world to California Chrome and all his connections. A group that included a formerly invisible but still humble exercise rider who still had a job to do whether anyone was paying attention or not.

ANIMALS OF ALL SPECIES COMING OUT FOR A LOOK AT CALIFORNIA CHROME (FRIDAY MAY 23)

The rapid rise to fame for California Chrome and anyone associated with his greatness leading up to and including the Belmont Stakes, was not limited just to the human population apparently. Despite a range of potential challengers who eagerly awaited their chance to knock off California Chrome in the Belmont not showing any interest in the Triple Crown story, it appeared that some other mammal species had no issues in checking out what all the hoopla was about.

Take the Thursday after California Chrome arrived at Belmont Park as prime evidence. While engaged in a bath after a light morning jog, television cameras focused in on a feral cat who decided to check out California Chrome getting all cleaned up. Ironically the cat was the same orange and white colors that California Chrome possessed Than things got a bit more weird three days later when an opossum decided to enter into a self-made race with California Chrome as the latter was out for another early jog.

As California Chrome galloped around the track in his 1 3/4 mile work, the opossum took a path along the right side of his opponent, gamely running for around half of the workout. Adding to the comedy of the "duel" between the two was video which surfaced later on in the day that showed the opossum in question first appearing on the other side of the track where California Chrome was running.

In a determined set of moves, the opossum noticeably began to dart in and out around the other horses out on the track that morning in his attempt to reach the star of the show. Despite the presence of the distracting opossum, Alan Sherman claimed that his colt was not bothered in the least by the intruder when meeting with reporters afterward. "It didn't faze him. We get coyotes in California all the time so it was no big deal. The track was a little heavier than it was yesterday but he seemed to handle it fine." If there were any doubt about the crazed attention centering around anything and everything to do with California Chrome, media outlets from all over the nation began calling in droves looking for any kind of video of the encounter. In addition a Twitter handle popped up dedicated to the opossum (@TheBelmontOposs) which added more ridiculousness to the whole day.

Of course the race was still paramount among everyone's minds and a few days after Danza pulled out of the Belmont, the rest of the field was still taking shape. As of Friday, May 23rd, 12 names were still on the board as possible challengers which would set a record with regards to the size of a field challenging a horse going for a Triple Crown. Among those still in line were Ride on Curlin (second in Preakness), Commanding Curve (second in Derby), Candy Boy, Tonalist, Intense Holiday, Kid Cruz, Ring Weekend, Matuszak, Wicked Strong, Samraat, and Social Inclusion. With all having scheduled workouts in the next few days, the field would soon start taking more firm shape based on their respective

results.

NO SIGN OF CALIFORNIA CHROME'S OPOSSUM RIVAL, ANOTHER CONTENDER WITHDRAWS (SATURDAY MAY 24)

A day after the spirited duel between California Chrome and the determined opossum that broke through security to land on the track, it was back to business as usual the Saturday of Memorial Day weekend. Willie Delgado got Chrome out for another early-morning jog on the sloppy main track, as rain continued to fall off and on. Alan Sherman, still running the show with Art not planning to come to New York until Tuesday at the earliest, saw California Chrome run at a moderate pace early on before ramping up the speed towards the end of the workout. "That's the way he gallops all the time. He kind of loafs the first mile and then he decides 'OK, let's get serious,' and gets into the bridle and pulls Willie around there." Still nothing out of the ordinary for California Chrome who got his bath right after the run back in Barn 26. Sherman did say however that Victor Espinoza would make a special trip to New York to get a half-mile workout in before the big race.

In related news, another contender dropped out of the Belmont which left 11 potential challengers. Graham Motion decided to skip the event with his Preakness loser Ring Weekend. Sherman however refused to comment on any of the goings-on with the rest of the challengers and instead continued to worry about California Chrome's well-being. "Three races in five weeks are tough on them. I'm not saying

Chrome can do it easier than any other horses who didn't. If he's good enough, he'll get it done."

INTENSE HOLIDAY INJURED IN WORKOUT, YET ANOTHER TOP CHALLENGER BOWS OUT (SUNDAY MAY 25)

Talk amongst the media gathered in Elmont on a hazy morning to see California Chrome's latest workout the Sunday before Memorial Day centered on the third withdrawal in three days for the Belmont Stakes which was now just two weeks away. While Danza was a prominent name that fell by the wayside, the mediocre Ring Weekend's defection 24 hours earlier didn't move the news needle much. However that was all about to change early in the day as it was learned that Todd Pletcher's prime Belmont Stakes contender Intense Holiday, suffered a non-displaced fracture of his right foreleg during his morning workout around the main track. Surgery would need to be performed the next day but Pletcher vowed that Intense Holiday's life was not in danger. "I don't think it's career-ending. It's particularly frustrating because after the Derby we ran tests and everything indicated he was healthy and ready to move forward. It's unfortunate."

Despite finishing 12th in the Derby, a rested Intense Holiday was universally considered to be one of the most potent challengers for California Chrome in the Belmont. Pletcher even made it a point to uncharacteristically speak about how off-the-charts Intense Holiday's workouts had been at Churchill Downs leading up the injury, which was an opinion shared by many who also saw him out on the track. However Intense Holiday's injury and the suddenness of his withdrawal was another reminder of just how fragile the body (and especially the legs) or a racehorse can be. The unspoken thought from anyone associated with California Chrome was that "this could happen to us" at a moment's notice like it did for Pletcher. A Triple Crown attempt could go up in smoke with just one false step or movement, as the owners of Spectacular Bid could tell you. And for Pletcher, the loss of Intense Holiday for the Belmont was his second big blow in less than a week since he also trained Danza. With now three possible challengers out of the running, the once-packed field for the Belmont was being whittled down to a possible 10.

Meanwhile California Chrome kept focused on his own work, running free and easy during his morning workout. Alan Sherman was particularly effusive in his praise for California Chrome later on in the day as he noted his colt "just keeps getting stronger. I can see it in his stride and the way he's taking hold of Willie that he seems to like this track. He's actually put on some weight since the Preakness. He looks so good right now." With dad Art prepared to meet up with the team in about a week, things were getting a bit more serious regarding California Chrome's preparation. As everything else was falling apart around him.

JUST ANOTHER DAY AT THE RACETRACK (MONDAY MAY 26)

It was a ridiculously early 6:00 AM on Memorial Day but California Chrome had no time to indulge in the holiday with a barbecue or a swim in the pool. Instead he was led out onto the Belmont Park main track by Willie Delgado for a two-mile gallop, which would turn out as routine and more importantly without incident like the ones prior. With his days as the trainer-in-chief dwindling with dad coming into town soon, Alan Sherman once again met with the early arriving media who couldn't get enough information on his colt. "The track was a little deeper today but he got over it fine," was Sherman's take on California Chrome's workout for the day. He also went on to note how California Chrome was taking to the Belmont track much better and quicker than he did at Churchill Downs where of course he won the Kentucky Derby drawing away.

Soon conversation steered toward Art Sherman and the fact he was still not in town with the Belmont Stakes now less than two weeks away. Alan Sherman reiterated that his father was kept abreast of every single detail concerning California Chrome and that nothing untoward had taken place. Instead more talk began to percolate regarding who was left to challenge California Chrome, what with Intense Holiday, Danza, and Ring Weekend all pulling out in he last few days. Bill Mott confirmed that his horse Matuszak would "absolutely" be running despite his terrible 1-for-8 record. Meanwhile Social Inclusion's owner Ron Sanchez hemmed on whether he would bring his horse to the Belmont or in the Met Mile

undercard race. It had started to get to the point where California Chrome's

workouts were getting a bit boring to cover for the media and instead the rumors

about who would be running against him became more interesting to speculate on.

RACING ROYALTY HOLDING COURT (TUESDAY MAY 27)

With California Chrome's Triple Crown attempt now just a week-and-a-half away, the media was now arriving in full force at Belmont Park from all across the country in order to cover every morsel of the upcoming attempt at history. Also historically anytime a Triple Crown had been at stake since Affirmed last completed the achievement in 1978, the media took the opportunity to check in with his aging connections in order to get their thoughts on the chances of another horse joining the immortal club. Adding to all the hype surrounding California Chrome, Affirmed's owner Patrice Wolfson and jockey Steve Cauthen were so besieged by media requests that they thought it best to hold one big conference call in order to pacify all who were interested in discussing the equine story of the year. While Wolfson had always spoken proudly in the past about her role as an owner of one of the only 11 Triple Crown winners in history, on this day she made it a point to say she was ready to hand the mantle off to someone else as the newest "last champion" of racing.

"I think I'm about ready to give up being 'the last Triple Crown winner'," Wolfson said during the call. "Sometimes I think 'the last Triple Crown winner' is my name. I think having a horse like California Chrome going for it is wonderful. I think he has the potential to be a great horse and we'll be cheering for him."

Wolfson made it a point to say that she was in fact planning to show up for the Belmont Stakes in person in order to possibly witness history and Cauthen echoed that sentiment when asked directly himself. "I think of all of them, California Chrome has the best chance. He's unique and has that excitement. Let's hope he shows it next Saturday." Cauthen meanwhile chose to focus in on the rides that Victor Espinoza had given California Chrome, one generation of jockey praising another. "I think he and California Chrome have a great relationship. It reminds me of Affirmed. This horse also can rate or go to the lead if he has to."

Meanwhile joining Wolfson and Cauthen on the conference call was Secretariat's owner Penny Chenery, who at 92 also vowed to be at the Belmont Stakes despite her advancing age. "I wasn't going to come because I'm getting up in years but if this horse wins the Triple Crown, I want to be there." The one thing Wolfson, Cauthen, and Chenery all agreed on is that California Chrome had the "It" factor that some other contenders in the past lacked. However Cauthen did throw a bit of caution to the wind in summing up the whole event. "California Chrome looks like a freak who can probably do things beyond his breeding. I'm pretty optimistic he has a great chance to pull it off. But Big Brown looked like a lock too, so you never know. That's why they run the races."

The gathering of Wolfson, Cauthen, and Chenery was also a prime opportunity for the media to pick their brains about the current state of racing. In noting the stark differences between racing back in the days of their champion colt's as opposed to the era that California Chrome was running in, Chenery brought up the often-discussed issue of training and breeding. "Well we don't breed horses for stamina so much these days and we don't train horses to run so frequently. Today's horse will run maybe six times a year. We're asking these 3-year-olds to run three times in five weeks, at different distances and at different racetracks. There are unfamiliar settings for the jockeys so you lose home advantage." Wolfson jumped right on board with Chenery's take in claiming that "I think the horses years ago were tougher, they campaigned harder, and they usually relished racing. They loved to run, particularly these Triple Crown winners of the 70's."

Another hot topic that quickly made the rounds was the growing chorus who claimed that the traditional setup of the Triple Crown series was no longer adequate for the current era of horse racing, an assertion that was voiced forcefully a year ago by Hall of Fame trainer D. Wayne Lukas. Lukas argued that the three respective races which make up the Triple Crown pursuit should be shortened a quarter of a mile each and he would also go to say that the traditional format "just doesn't work anymore." As respected as Lukas is in the racing industry, he would find no supporters among Chenery, Wolfson, and Cauthen. "I'm just against that. I'm a traditionalist and that's my only answer. I think it would invalidate all of the records and all of the times and make it an entirely different event. I guess the feeling is that since it hasn't been won for so long, people will lose interest in it but that just makes it a more interesting challenge." Wolfson slammed Lukas' idea of changing the distances and other ideas of spacing the races out. "That would be just awful. It's a wonderful and unique set of races and if they changed it, it would not work." Finally Cauthen was short and to the point when he stated "If you change it, it's not the same. It doesn't count." Clearly tradition still ruled the day for this trio and it became crystal clear that any type of change would destroy the pursuit in a very negative way.

In moving back to the racetrack, the talk of the day Wednesday among the media horde was how California Chrome continued to tear it up all around Big Sandy. Unlike at Churchill Downs and at Pimlico, it was obvious to anyone who could see that California Chrome was absolutely loving the track. This was confirmed later by Willie Delgado after their two-mile jog on a very warm day at Belmont Park. "He was so much stronger today. He was pulling me and I had to pull him back. This is the strongest he's felt and he really gets over the track well. I just hope he can keep going and win in the Triple Crown. Then I can retire."

AND THEN THERE WERE THREE! (WEDNESDAY MAY 28)

Back when Affirmed became the 11th horse to win the Triple Crown (the last of three in the 1970's plus Seattle Slew's close call in '79), the sport of horse racing would almost be unrecognizable to trainers, runners, and the star attractions themselves. While horses today come close to measuring up to their earlier ancestors with regards to the size and timed speed, the one stark difference that is obvious even to lukewarm fans is the sharp decline in racing frequency from today's top colts and fillies. With stud and breeding riches skyrocketing to unfathomable heights, racing a prized horse is simply not worth the risk of injury for trainers and especially their owners. So while Triple Crown champions like Whirlaway would run an unheard of by today's standards 60 times in his career, even those runners who fell just short from completing the trifecta in the Belmont Stakes like Smarty Jones and Big Brown were retired right after their defeat so as not to jeopardize their post-racing value.

In addition to the lack of overall running by today's top horses, another interesting development over the last decade or so had taken place in the Triple Crown series itself. While any horse who has even the most minute amount of talent fights tooth and nail to be among one of the 20 entrants in the very crowded Kentucky Derby, often only the champion and maybe one or two others will go on to race in the Preakness two weeks later. The rest of Churchill Downs' vanquished foes instead go back into training in order to prep for the Belmont Stakes a full five weeks later. Having the fresher horse with a much improved chance of victory as opposed to one who might be tired from racing for the third time in five weeks, had become the preferred method of racing for those who failed to win the Derby. Thus the freshened up Empire Maker's, Sarava's, and Birdstone's of the world have come out with big races in the Belmont Stakes at the expense of those chasing the Triple Crown dream while on fumes.

It was this such a story that presented itself leading up to the California Chrome's attempt to win the Belmont Stakes on June 7th in his quest to become the sport's 12th Triple Crown winner. With California Chrome facing his third grueling race in five weeks, the concern regarding his Triple Crown candidacy was whether or not he had anything left to conquer the unending mile-and-a-half Big Sandy. However since arriving at Belmont Park just a few days after winning the Preakness, California Chrome was doing his best to show anyone with a pair of eyes that this concern was a non-factor as far as he was concerned. Once again the talk of the media contingent on hand for California Chrome's 2-mile exercise ride around the main track that early Thursday morning was how he continually was tearing it up in his workouts, running with a relative ease maybe not seen since Affirmed. Also once again Willie Delgado couldn't hide his excitement about the freshness of his colt. "He was pulling me around which show's he's feeling real good. When he pulled up, he wasn't breathing hard enough to blow out a match. Fitness-wise he's fine. He's gained weight and is sharper than he was before the Derby. He didn't like the track at Churchill but he liked Pimlico and he loves this one." Delgado was confirming what was obvious to all, which was that California Chrome was bucking all the preconceived negative trends that almost all Triple Crown contenders faced with regards to stamina. There was no apparent hint of fatigue and Delgado's statement about how California Chrome didn't like Churchill Downs' track but yet still ran to an easy victory in the Derby was startling. With Victor Espinoza due in on the Saturday before the race, final preparations were in full swing.

In addition to California Chrome, who had a certain reason to run in all three legs of the Triple Crown, there was only one two other horses in the series who would join him in running in all three races. After finishing a rallying seventh in the Derby after getting squeezed early in the race along the rail, Ride on Curlin looked poised to end the Triple Crown dreams of California Chrome at Pimlico when he came up along his opponent's shoulders in the stretch which led trainer Billy Gowan to think they were about to enter the winner's circle. "At the eighth pole I thought I had a shot. And that was after he was steadied twice." California Chrome fought back gamely though and eventually put Ride on Curlin away after a short but spirited duel. Still Gowan had seen enough for him to send Ride on

Curlin to the Belmont and it was the son of two-time Horse of the Year Curlin who was universally looked at as one the top threats to California Chrome's Triple Crown hopes. Also in a nod to how racing used to be, Gowan admitted he never thought twice of running Ride on Curlin in all three legs of the Triple Crown. "He only ran an eighth of a mile (in the Derby) and the next day he was bouncing around the barn. That's when I started thinking about the Preakness. People told me 'No, you should rest him and wait for the Belmont. You don't want to run in all three races. Back in the day, that's all they did." According to Gowan, it was fitting that both Ride on Curlin and California Chrome were the two favorites in the upcoming Belmont. A major criticism of racing in it's present state were the arguments that the top horses simply don't run enough anymore to bring attention to the sport like in the old days. At least for the 2014 Triple Crown series, both California Chrome and Ride on Curlin were doing their best to bring a bit of the past to the present. They would be joined by General A Rod in all three legs of the series.

The last remaining bit of news on the day was the late addition of Dale Romans' Medal Count to the Belmont Stakes field. After running eighth in the Derby, Romans indicated he loved the way Medal Count was looking on the racetrack and that a big race was in his future. With the field still far from set, Medal Count's inclusion at least stopped the recent trend of withdrawals, much to the chagrin of

all California Chrome fans everywhere.

BILLY GOWAN STILL TALKING BIG, JOINED BY DALLAS STEWART

When it came to the positive impact that a modern-day Triple Crown winner would have on the sport of horse racing, trainers of the respective entrants who would try and prevent California Chrome from completing the trick no doubt thought differently. Just a day after Preakness runner-up Ride on Curlin's trainer Billy Gowan spoke of his desire to go all-out in his effort to knock off California Chrome, he was joined in the chorus by Dallas Stewart whose colt Commanding Curve finished second in the Derby. Much is still made in racing circles about the unspoken but strongly perceived tag-team duo of retired jockey Jerry Bailey and the still-active Gary Stevens working together to thwart Smarty Jones' attempt to win the Triple Crown back in 2004 and whether or not such a scenario could repeat itself at the expense of California Chrome. While no trainer or jockey involved in the upcoming race would bite on that controversy, what became crystal clear is that no one was going to hand California Chrome the Triple Crown either.

"It's going to take a really good horse to beat him. If I can do it, I won't be too upset. I'll be elated to tell you the truth", explained Gowan. Stewart meanwhile was a little more subdued but generally agreed with Gowan's take. "That's a tough question to answer. Our job is to go out there and win horse races. Sure if California Chrome does win, it's great for horse racing. But if we won, I don't think it would hurt horse racing."

As had been the case since his arrival at the Belmont Park racetrack, California Chrome was oblivious to the chaos around him. After his early pre-7:00 A.M. workout on a cool Thursday morning, California Chrome checked out the Belmont Park paddock for the first time with Willie Delgado and Alan Sherman. "I don't know if it was the weather but he was pretty happy today, "reported Sherman. "As usual he started off slowly but when he hit the half-mile pole he started going pretty good." Sherman again discussed the arrival of Victor Espinoza Saturday for California Chrome's only timed workout before the race and how everyone involved in his preparation expressed not even a nary of concern about their star. With the week prior to the Belmont Stakes serving as the launching point for the arrival of the national media, things were about to get a whole lot more crazed for a group looking for nothing but serenity despite the magnitude of the moment getting closer by the day.

TIME FOR SOME NEW SHOES (FRIDAY MAY 30)

Perhaps sensing that something big was happening around him on a scale growing with each passing day, California Chrome woke up Friday morning feeling extra frisky and full of energy. With the monotony of nine straight days of just galloping around the main track at Belmont Park maybe not doing enough to unleash his pent up fuel, Alan Sherman was struck by how his colt was "climbing out of his skin" early that morning. Sherman could easily see that California Chrome was "ready to work" and in just 24 hours he would be reunited with his jockey who was coming in on a red eye flight from the West Coast for their scheduled Saturday prep. It was a meeting that Sherman was looking forward to due to his belief that "once Victor gets on him, he'll know it's time to work."

The exercise with Espinoza was already going to be a circus, what with CBS, NBC, Fox, and ABC all having camera crews and reporters slated to show up before dawn in order to witness the event. Clearly getting used to the massive influx of media descending on Belmont Park on a daily basis, Sherman had no reaction when asked about whether or not it was distracting to California Chrome's training. Instead Sherman was more interested in the time that California Chrome was going to put forth with Espinoza once again in the saddle and he admitted that "if he works in 48 seconds and gallops out in 1:01, that would be perfect."

Before Espinoza's arrival however, the task at hand for Sherman Friday was to get California Chrome into the Belmont Park starting gate in order to get him acclimated to the dimensions and its look. Sherman had spoken a few times prior about how California Chrome grows a bit anxious in the starting gate, especially if the loading takes extra time to complete. He talked about how California Chrome at other times also "has a tendency to spread his feet in there and rock back and forth. I might take him one more time next week."

In addition to the prep work with the starting gate, California Chrome also had a date with personal blacksmith Judd Farrier who planned to put new shoes onto his hoofs. Yet another unheralded but important part of the California Chrome team, Farrier had installed new shoes onto the colt prior to his winning run in the Preakness. Farrier would nail the new shoes into California Chrome's feet, a bit of an awkward thought due to the delicate nature of the exercise. As the ownership of Spectacular Bid could tell you, a simple stepped on pin sometimes is all it takes to derail a Triple Crown dream. Sherman however had nothing but praise for Farrier and reiterated that "I trust Judd's judgment. He doesn't tell me how to do my job and I don't tell him how to do his." All part of the partnership from all angles that had gotten California Chrome to the doorstep of greatness.

VICTOR ESPINOZA BACK IN TOWN, GENERAL A ROD WANTS A PIECE (SATURDAY MAY 31)

Despite the incredibly early start to the day, the media contingent awaiting the star attraction as the sun barely rose up from the sky the Saturday before the Belmont Stakes was immense. Field reporters, video cameras, and journalists from all over the country had already staked out their spots along the perimeter of the Belmont Park main track for the one and only timed workout of California Chrome under the guidance of his jockey Victor Espinoza. After Espinoza arrived early that morning on a red eye from California, he quietly led his colt out onto the track as cameras clicked from all directions.

Sensing the moment at hand, California Chrome proceeded to do what he always did best as a runner. Which was to leave mouths agape as he breezed around the track in a scorching 47.69 for a half-mile. Among the large swell of media witnessing the workout was The Daily Racing Form's Mike Vesce who came over with timed watch in hand. His reaction after the sprint was completed could have summed up the collective response from the rest of the crowd. "Off that work, he's going to be tough to beat. I think we're going to have a Triple Crown winner and I didn't think that before." Meanwhile Alan Sherman himself was failing miserably at trying to hide his glee. "It was a great work, exactly what we wanted. It was great to have the fans come out to see him. Victor said he went great and that he was very happy with him." In addition to the workout, Sherman also was finally able to confirm that father Art would arrive early Monday morning from Los Alamitos. As far as Espinoza was concerned, he too would be very busy as he planned to stay in New York through the Belmont. His itinerary included throwing out the first pitch before Monday's New York Yankees game at the Stadium and sitting down with David Lettermen on "Late Show" Wednesday.

Once the prep work was complete, California Chrome stayed true to his schedule of getting a full bath. Privacy was in short supply though as the media horde followed his every move. Not feeling bashful in the least, California Chrome looked like he was enjoying the attention, at one point appearing like he was posing for the cameras.

In summing up the day, both Espinoza and Alan Sherman had nothing but praise for California Chrome's latest workout gem. "He looked great. He handled the track very well. I think he likes the surface at Belmont" was Espinoza's take. Since he was out of town up until that point, Espinoza had no clue about the prevailing proclamation that California Chrome was in love with Big Sandy.

California Chrome was not the only Belmont runner or potential runner to get in a workout at the park that day. Tonalist, Social Inclusion, Samraat , and Medal Count all put in solid runs. With General A Rod also now in the fold, the Belmont Stakes field was back around the expected 10 or 11 entrants. Despite the dominance of California Chrome, no one seemed to be shying away from the challenge of trying to derail his Triple Crown hopes. Based on the workout California Chrome put forth on the day however, their chances surely didn't look promising.

REUNITED AT LAST, SOCIAL INCLUSION ANXIETY-RIDDEN (Monday June 2)

Perhaps the fastest dash of the day at Belmont Park on the Monday before the big race was performed not by a horse but by a human being. A 77-year-old one at that. A black stretch limo pulled up outside Belmont Park in mid-morning and out stepped an overexcited Art Sherman, fresh off returning to the metro area after two weeks overseeing his stable in Los Alamitos, California. Sherman had only one thing on this mind that morning and it certainly wasn't his coffee or newspaper. Instead upon exiting the limo, Sherman immediately undertook a very brisk walk/jog straight to Bar 26, Stall 7 in order to reunite with California Chrome whom the trainer had not seen since shortly after their victorious run in the Preakness Stakes.

Perhaps not recognizing his trainer at first, California Chrome tried to bite Sherman's outstretched hand as the reunion got underway. No matter to Sherman who was just happy to see his horse again after so much time spent away from one another. "You miss him," the grinning Sherman exclaimed. "He looks great. The horse looks good. I go by his stall back in California all the time and I see it's empty. It kinda makes me feel funny." In response to one inquiry about California Chrome's odd attempt at a greeting after the bite attempt, Sherman didn't miss a beat. "I know he's all right because he tried to bite me right away. I didn't have a cookie for him (California Chrome's favorite snack was Mrs. Pastures Cookies) and he was like 'Hey, what's with it?"

With the Belmont Stakes now just a few days away, Sherman said he would do his best to take in the scenery and pageantry of the event despite the work that remained for Saturday. In addition, Sherman also revealed his superstitious side during his Monday news conference when discussing the "boatloads" of fan mail he and California Chrome had received on a daily basis since winning the Derby. "I got this one lucky dollar that one gal gave me. Before the Derby she gave me this dollar (pulling it out of a wad of cash) and she said 'You're going to win the Triple Crown with this dollar.' So that's not leaving my side right there. I'll never spend that dollar."

Joining Sherman a bit later in the day was Steve Coburn and his wife Carolyn, who arrived at the track for the first time as they too reunited with California Chrome. Throughout the whole Triple Crown series, Coburn continued to serve as the face of ownership while the media-shy Perry Martin remained secluded. Coburn had no such anxiety around reporters and television cameras however and once again channeled his inner Nostradamus in discussing California Chrome's chances for Saturday. "There's no doubt in my mind he's going to win the Triple Crown. Because I've seen him perform the other two times and his looks this past Saturday tell me this horse is healthy, he's happy. He's gaining weight and putting on muscle. He's ready to go."

After taking a rest a day earlier, California Chrome was back out on the track early Monday under Willie Delgado as they galloped for a mile-and-a-half with no issues, which was followed by the customary bath and hay snacking. Meanwhile on the same track that morning, the story was not as positive for Ron Sanchez' colt Social Inclusion. Just a few days after Social Inclusion raised eyebrows with a blistering 3 furlong work in 33:48, Sanchez acknowledged to reporters Monday that the Belmont Stakes was now looking doubtful by a "70/30" margin due to a strong case of "anxiety" impacting his colt. Specifically, Sanchez noted that Social Inclusion had a disastrous training session that morning while practicing being loaded into the starting gate, which was an issue at the Preakness two weeks earlier.

Just prior to the Preakness getting underway, Social Inclusion was a ball of nerves and agitation on such a high level that he became noticeably covered in sweat. In addition, right after being loaded into the starting gate, Social Inclusion reared up and almost flipped completely over with jockey Luis Contreras aboard. After a rough start to the race where he didn't get the lead for the first time in his promising career, Social Inclusion rallied late to move right up alongside California Chrome at the top of the stretch but all the sweating and nervousness likely took hold there as he finished a dull fourth. Despite the setback, Sanchez was unbowed afterwards. "I'm proud of my horse and for now, we're going to the Belmont." The words "for now" gave Sanchez the option to pull Social Inclusion if things didn't go well in training and it was that exact scenario that was unfolding right before his eyes with the race days away. "We have time. We are going to do what's best for the horse. There are a lot of good races coming up."

The big issue Sanchez explained was the fact that the loading gate at the start of the Belmont Stakes was located directly in front of the stands. Stands that figured to be jam packed with a record crowd on hand to see California Chrome's attempt to win the Triple Crown. Thus there was major concern that Social Inclusion would once again act up badly and possibly get injured. If Social Inclusion was in fact withdrawn like Sanchez seemed to suggest, his removal would eliminate a good bit of early speed from the Belmont Stakes which once again would only help California Chrome's chances.

With the post position draw set for Wednesday, the field would finally be confirmed and all conjecture about possible challengers would be put to rest.

STEVE COBURN HOLDS COURT

Whenever there has been a Triple Crown on the line, the Tuesday before the Belmont Stakes has always been known as the unofficial "media day." Where trainers, owners, and anyone else noteworthy associated with the expected field holds court with print and television reporters looking for any nugget of information that already hadn't been covered. For the connections of California Chrome, the media blitz would be unrelenting, what with Art Sherman having now finally arrived in town the day before. However the main attraction of the day would be the always colorful Steve Coburn who once again served as the face of ownership with Perry Martin choosing to remain behind the scenes. Continuing to show his knack for the colorful quotes and opinionated answers that make headline writers' jobs easy, Coburn stole the show.

Alternating between moody and cheerful depending on the topic, Coburn didn't leave a stone unturned when it came to his thoughts on all of the respective topics thrown his way. Regarding the circus surrounding him, Coburn showed the media no love. "It's a black eye. Everything's gotta be a big theatrical performance." A reporter quickly followed up with a question about the state of racing which again Coburn had a firm response for. "The horse racing industry these days is going down. We're just trying to bring a little fun back in the game. We're just a couple of good ol' boys having a good time and we're just doing everything we can to do all the publicity. But it could be a lot easier than they actually make it."

Eventually the topic turned to California Chrome who Coburn couldn't stop gushing about. Describing him as "America's horse," Coburn explained why the public had grown so attached to his colt in such a short time span. "He became really attached to people. He really loves people. If you'll notice, if you're holding up a camera. he'll stop. He'll let you take his picture." Eventually Coburn grew visibly weary of holding court, finishing up his portion of the press conference by summing up California Chrome's chances on Saturday. "Yes I do expect him to win. I really do. All right guys. Now I gotta get something to eat." With that Coburn moved toward the expansive buffet table set up in the Rockefeller Center rooftop plaza where the media luncheon was taking place.

In moving around the vast array of horse racing personalities during the media session, it became clear that the chief topic of the day was A: Whether California Chrome could become the 12th Triple Crown winner and B: What a Triple Crown could do for the fledgling sport. Perhaps the most expressive on the topic was retired jockey Richard Migliore who was always a popular interview during his racing days. Migliore opined that while a Triple Crown attempt brings much-needed attention to the sport, a victory was long overdue. "If you think back to Smarty Jones and how the air went out of the building when he was caught by

Birdstone, the disappointment. Now it's kind of turned in a cynical way to, 'It's never going to happen again.' I really think, 36 years since Affirmed did it, we need a horse to do it, to prove it actually can be done. I think we're past the point now where it's just a buildup. People want to see it. People are starting to lose faith that it can be done."

Standing close by to Migliore, was Hall of Fame jockey Jerry Bailey who concurred with his former racing foe. "The longer you go without it, the more attempts it takes without success, I guess the anticipation does go up. That's a valid point. But I'm going to go on the side of thinking it's better for racing that we finally actually get it done." Migliore brought up the often-discussed topic of changing the Triple Crown system given the 36-year drought; an idea that was championed by D. Wayne Lukas who used to employ him as one of his main riders. "It's 36 years and we're back to talk that it's too hard; they should make it easier. I almost feel it's enough already. I just really want it to happen."

Migliore's opinion was shared by not just those associated with horse racing but by the general public as well. With all the buildup that takes place in the three weeks between the Preakness and the Belmont Stakes, the fallout from a failed Triple Crown bid has served as a collective shot to the gut for all who sat on the edges of their seats pining for a new addition to the champion's club. With each Real Quiet or Smarty Jones close call; or Big Brown and I'll Have Another no-show (both on and off the track), the jaded nature of the public regarding whether a horse can win the Triple Crown in the current setup was an issue that had increasingly taken on a life of its own.

Meanwhile in his first full day in Elmont, Art Sherman was not interested in joining the Migliore/Bailey debate about the Triple Crown effect. Instead Sherman reiterated what he had already said countless times prior which was that his horse had everything he needed to join the Triple Crown champions club Saturday. "He's a horse who carries his flesh well and has a certain air about him. He has the urge to compete and he's ready to rock and roll. If he wins the Belmont, it would be the top of the world for me and the whole team."

In addition to discussing California Chrome, Sherman also took the opportunity to engage reporters about his past connections to New York City and in particular Belmont Park. "I didn't remember Belmont being this big. I enjoyed riding it because it had a nice surface and I liked the big turns. It's beautiful and it's good to be back." With a great deal of New York-area reporters amongst the gathering, Sherman continued to show he still had a knack for saying what everyone gathered around him wanted to hear. "I'm kind of a city guy. New York has always been a fun town for me. I remember when I was riding that there was a lot of action when I was a young feller." Finally in discussing his past connection to the heavily Jewish community of Williamsburg, Sherman claimed that "They tell me it's changed. I can afford it now."

BELMONT STAKES POST POSITION DRAW

At a grueling mile-and-a-half, a distance that no horse in the Belmont Stakes field had ever run or would ever run again, the bigger issue was not where he would start from but where he would end up when the race was in the final stretch. Being that the distance was so lengthy, it was accepted that a jockey riding around Big Sandy had enough time to work through any traffic issues that cropped up and in turn not allow any post position to greatly impact the result. Endurance was the name of the game in the Belmont Stakes which for California Chrome was the only concern remaining for his ownership and Art Sherman. While they professed full confidence in California Chrome's chance to win any given duel, the three-races-in-five-weeks schedule was always focused on as the main danger to his Triple Crown denial. Thus when California Chrome drew the number 2 post, a collective shrug was shared by the present Sherman and Steve Coburn. Installed as the 3-5 favorite, California Chrome would officially be challenged by 10 other horses.

"Going a mile and a half, it's a good post position," Sherman said. "At least you can save some ground and see who's going to have the speed and where you'll land going into the first turn. It's going to be a jockeys' race anyhow, so it's up to Victor to ride the race the way he's been riding. I can't predict who's going to go for the lead, but I don't see him being any farther back than third on the backstretch."

Meanwhile it was quickly pointed out that Secretariat also came out of the number two post in his epic romp to the Triple Crown.

As far as the rest of the field was concerned Wicked Strong would be the second choice at 6-1 out of the nine post while Peter Pan winner Tonalist would go off at 8-1 from post 11. The field of 11 didn't include either Social Inclusion and Kid Cruz, as the owners of each decided their colts were not up for the challenge. Finally, only General A Rod and Ride On Curlin joined California Chrome in running in all three legs of the series. No matter who was in the field, Coburn was unimpressed.

"It's been a tremendous ride, and it's all coming to the top of the Triple Crown pyramid," Coburn said. "He's an amazing animal, one in a bazillion. He could have been born to anyone, but he was born to us. I think we have America on our side, except for these people who are running their horses against us. I hope that after the Belmont they come on board."

The official field for the Belmont Stakes:

1 -- Medal Count (20-1)

2 -- California Chrome (3-5)

3 -- Matterhorn (30-1)

4 -- Commanding Curve (15-1)

5 -- Ride On Curlin (12-1)

6 -- Matuszak (30-1)

7 -- Samraat (20-1)

8 -- Commissioner (20-1)

9 -- Wicked Strong (6-1)

10 -- General a Rod (20-1)

11 -- Tonalist (8-1)

While the California Chrome corner was clearly the center of attention at the Belmont Stakes draw, the New York-centric media began to exploit another ready-made story for the hometown folks. At 20-1 out of the 7 post, Kentucky Derby fifth place finisher Samraat served as a bit of a local flavor story given the fact he was foaled at My Meadowview Farm out in Water Mill, Long Island which was just a train ride away. While owner Len Riggio made it a point to show respect for the ability and impressive accomplishments of California Chrome, he also reveled in possibly playing the spoiler role. "Well I'm rooting for Samraat. There's a lot of people rooting for Samraat. Everyone I know is crazy for Samraat. He's the most lovable horse I know."

While it was easy to pick up on the tongue-in-cheek act Riggio was putting on for reporters, it also became obvious just how much confidence he had in his colt. "He's the most intelligent horse I've ever known. He's also the kindest and the toughest." Riggio's positivity was also echoed by Samraat's trainer Rick Violette. "I don't think anybody in the race is going to say a mile-and-a-half on the dirt is their strength. But I don't think we would have changed a day or a stride. Everything has been spot on."

The bottom line for Riggio and the other nine owners who were sending out a challenger to go up against California Chrome in the Belmont Stakes was winning. While all would likely admit to the likelihood of rooting for California Chrome to win the Triple Crown if they were just a fan and not invested into the race with a horse of their own, Riggio's take on focusing in on only his runner was all that would matter to him shortly after 6:50 on Saturday. "I don't mind being called a winner. And if what comes with it is becoming a spoiler, I'll remember the winner and you remember the spoiler."

NBC CREW TRYING TO STAY NEUTRAL (THURSDAY JUNE 5)

21.9 million. That staggering number was the tally of viewers who tuned into NBC back in 2004 to watch Smarty Jones' ultimately failed attempt to win the Triple Crown of racing at the Belmont Stakes, a number that was in serious jeopardy of being surpassed for California Chrome's shot at immortality on Saturday. Clearly understanding the enormity of what was in front of them, NBC would leave no stone unturned when it came to covering the race and all the themes that would go into it as evidenced by the 1,700 word-news release they sent out to all media outlets a few days prior.

Helping to cover every inch of the pageantry were NBC's stable of horse racing announcers and experts which included veteran studio anchor Tom Hammond, along with a who's who of well-known personalities ranging from retired Hall of Fame jockey Jerry Bailey, Derby linesmaker Mike Battaglia, and commentators Donna Brothers, Randy Moss, and Kenny Rice. Understanding the need to be partial with 10 other horses in the field, the crew admitted that the task was a bit difficult due to the thoughts surrounding how great a Triple Crown winner would be for horse racing and the day's ratings in general. "I'm really looking forward to it," said Hammond during a conference call the Thursday before the Belmont. "And while we won't be rooting, I would like in the rest of my lifetime at least to see a Triple Crown winner if we could and to cover one would be great."

Echoing Hammond's theme, Moss espoused that "We're not rooting, obviously, but having seen failures so often through so many years, we all would love at some point to see one of these horses pull it off. We all think California Chrome not only is a great story but he's in there with the fighting chance to pull it off. Maybe he's the one." It was classic spin doctoring by Hammond, Moss, and anyone else from NBC who spoke during the press briefing. Deep down they all knew the positive ramifications of what a Triple Crown could do for their sport and also how being the ones to anchor the coverage of California Chrome possibly getting crowned a champion would link them all professionally as part of sports television history.

Despite the obvious underlying meanings to their words, no one came out and said concretely they were pushing for California Chrome to win. However Bailey would the closest as the retired jockey was asked once again about spoiling the popular Funny Cide's bid back in 2003 with Empire Maker. "At that point in time my job was to try and win a race even if it included denying the horse a Triple Crown. But from this side of the fence I have the interest of what's best for the sport. To see it would be wonderful."

THE BELMONT STAKES/DATE WITH DESTINY

Even Perry Martin couldn't sit this one out. It was a little past noon on Belmont Stakes day when California Chrome's owners Martin and Steve Coburn filed into the park amid never-ending cheers from the more than 100,000 patrons who came to possibly witness history. While Coburn had become a sizable celebrity in his own right during California Chrome's Triple Crown chase due to his resemblance to actor Wilfred Brimley and his outspoken demeanor, the fact that Martin showed up as well spoke volumes as to the magnitude of the day. Martin had been almost completely absent from the public eye since the Kentucky Derby due to the anxiety he suffered from the massive crowd that day and subsequently in the weeks since California Chrome won the first two legs of the Triple Crown. Despite Martin's presence, Coburn remained the voice of the California Chrome team.

As he signed some autographs as he filed into the park, Coburn quickly began his give-and-take with the monstrous media contingent on hand. "We need this (a Triple Crown) for horse racing, in the world, not only the United States. We need this. America needs a Triple Crown winner. They really, really do in a very, very bad way, and I'm just fortunate to be part owner in a horse that's going to get it done today." Clearly Coburn's supreme confidence in California Chrome had not wavered one bit, nor did his knack for being a reporter's dream.

As far as the star attraction was concerned, California Chrome remained in his stall for most of the day, oblivious to the circus going on all around him on the bright, sun-splashed day. Unlike Coburn, Art and Alan Sherman also kept a low profile as the Belmont Stakes undercard made its way though the early races. With the Belmont Stakes beckoning, California Chrome became the 3-5 favorite as the betting public surely stocked up on potential winning ticket souvenirs.

Eventually the moment of truth was at hand as Frank Sinatra Jr. would have made his father proud by belting out a resounding rendition of "New York, New York" which followed the "Rider's Up" call by Affirmed's retired jockey Steve Cauthen. California Chrome and the rest of the 11-horse field began to make their way in order to the starting gate as the crowd roared in anticipation. Coburn meanwhile kissed his wife and sat down for a quick prayer next to Martin.

Once at the gate, California Chrome loaded with no issues, as did the other 10 entrants. With race announcer Larry Collmus setting the stage, the loudest cheer of the day went up as all were now locked and loaded. A split-second later the starting gates swung open and the run to Triple Crown glory began for California Chrome. A mile-and-a-half from destiny. A mile-and-a-half to immortality. A mile-and-a-half to possibly cementing his status as the "People's Horse" from now to eternity.

As with any race, getting out of the gate cleanly and without incident has always been considered the first hurdle to overcome. No one needed to remind Victor Espinoza of this after War Emblem stumbled to his knees coming out of the gate in his failed Belmont Stakes bid years earlier which finished him off not even a stride into the race.

It looked like that potential crisis was averted as California Chrome showed good early speed out of the gate despite a slight wobble his first few steps. Despite the solid start, the first surprise of the Belmont Stakes was quickly seen with Todd Pletcher's Commissioner gunning right to the front of the pack. Commissioner was not considered to be a candidate for the lead going into the first turn as he had failed to show such a burst in any of his previous races. However Commissioner went to the lead as the field approached the turn, passing California Chrome on the outside as Medal Count stayed packed along the rail in third. Tonalist meanwhile was slow getting into gear having to start from the outside post.

As they moved along the backstretch in approaching the half-mile mark, Commissioner continued to set the pace as General A Rod now moved into second. California Chrome sat in third in a very good stalking position near the rail. It was at this point where Tonalist began to find his stride, moving up on the outside to pass California Chrome for third place behind the still comfortable Commissioner and General A Rod. Meanwhile California Chrome was now encountering his first significant batch of trouble in the Triple Crown series as he became struck along the rail behind Commissioner, General A Rod, and Tonalist. In addition, California Chrome was noticeably getting dirt kicked into his face for the first time since prior to the Kentucky Derby, a development Art Sherman had been concerned with. Still the half-mile was run in a slow 48.52 which was the same exact scenario that played out in the Derby and Preakness which allowed California Chrome to save energy for a late surge. Only this time he would have to fight through some traffic and deal with the extra quarter mile around Big Sandy.

With the far turn now approaching, California Chrome was being passed by Medal Count as he dropped into fifth place. It was here where Espinoza decided to make a move, guiding California Chrome to the outside in order to escape the congestion along the rail. Espinoza would find himself and California Chrome four-wide as they continued to move around the far turn, not the most ideal spot with the very long homestretch beckoning. General A Rod had now passed Commissioner for the lead, with Tonalist moving strong on the outside of the two. California Chrome meanwhile had now launched his move, picking up steam as the field now began to enter the homestretch.

With the crowd eliciting a deafening roar as Larry Collmus announced "they are into the stretch," Commissioner had retaken the lead from General A Rod as Tonalist began to charge. California Chrome remained an unforgiving four wide as they settled for the run home. With 300 yards from the wire and Collmus exclaiming he was only a furlong from immortality, California Chrome appeared to be stalling as Commissioner opened up a tad more daylight on the lead, with Tonalist and now the late-closing Wicked Strong battling for second. Sensing the race was slipping away at this point, Sherman slapped his hands together in frustration as he realized California Chrome was not going to get there.

With even Collmus now acknowledging that California Chrome was out of the race, Tonalist surged forward as the wire neared to nip Commissioner for the win. California Chrome would dead-heat with Wicked Strong for fourth behind Tonalist, Commissioner, and Medal Count in that order. Despite the big victory, Joel Rosario's only outward satisfaction was to pat Tonalist on the side, nary a fist pump to be seen as the crowd grew stone dead silent. Meanwhile all Art Sherman could do was shake his head in disappointment as thousands began to file out of the park in stunned silence.

Just minutes after California Chrome's defeat, NBC's Kenny Rice quickly fought through the crowd to get a quick response from Coburn who was still visibly shocked at what he had just witnessed. While Rice had always been considered a solid sports contributor during NBC's run covering the Triple Crown series, little did he know that he was about to become a part of an instantly viral interview with a seething Coburn. The stage was set when Rice predictably asked

Coburn his initial thoughts on the race and what came next was a response so fiery and direct that it quickly overshadowed the Belmont Stakes itself. Once again reiterating what he had stated prior to the race about how horses who were not eligible for the Kentucky Derby should not be allowed to run in any of the three legs, Coburn exploded into sheer rage after being given the opening by Rice.

"This is the coward's way out. I'm 61 years old and in my lifetime, I'll never see another Triple Crown winner because of the way they do this. It's not fair to these horses that have been in the game since Day 1. If you don't make enough points to get into the Kentucky Derby, you can't run in the other two races. It's all or nothing. This is not fair to these horses and to the people that believe in them. This is the coward's way out in my opinion. This is the coward's way out."

It was at this point where Coburn's wife Carol, who was standing behind him, nudged the back of her husband as she could be heard saying "Stop it Steve!" in a clear attempt to get him to calm down. Still Rice kept at it, asking Coburn if California Chrome's challengers conspired together to deny him the crown. Once again Coburn took the bait and fired off by saying "Our horse had a target on his back and everybody lays out one and they won't run in the Kentucky Derby or the Preakness. They'll wait until the Belmont. If you've got a horse, (it was at this point where Carol Coburn nudged her husband a second time in order to get him to cease with the rant, only to be rebuffed with a backward nudge from his hand) run him in

95

all three. Those 20 horses that start in Kentucky are the only 20 eligible to run in all three races. This is the coward's way out."

With that Rice, perhaps sensing the temperature of the conversation was getting too high, cut the interview in sending it back to Tom Hammond. Coburn was than reprimanded one last time by his wife, which brought an angry "I don't care retort!" which the NBC cameras picked up clearly.

Whether it was sour grapes or bad sportsmanship by Coburn would be up for debate amongst all the television reporters and print media on hand after the quotes made their way into ever filed story on the Belmont Stakes. Meanwhile Espinoza was left to ponder how a second attempt to ride a Triple Crown winner went awry. "Turning for home, I was just waiting for him to have the same kick he always had before and today he was a little bit flat down the lane. He just didn't have it today. It was tough for him, he ran back-to-back races at different tracks. He was a little bit empty today." In response to a question as to whether California Chrome balked at being forced along the rail in close proximity to the other horses around him, Espinoza admitted "I noticed he got a little bit shy in there. It's tough to win this race. I wish I could explain it, why you know he didn't perform like before. But I feel like he was not really in this race today." Despite yet another close call to immortality, Espinoza continued to praise California Chrome and the golden chance he got as his jockey. "Regardless of what happened today, I believe he's one of the best horses I ever rode in my career and I had a tremendous, tremendous ride with him."

On the other side of the jockey ledger, Rosario continued to keep a low celebratory profile despite another major win in a career that was shaping him up as one of the best in the business. Regarding his role in spoiling the potential Triple Crown party, Rosario admitted his victory was bittersweet. "I'm a little bit upset about California Chrome. If I was going to get beat, I just wanted to get beat by him."

With Steve Coburn's post-race rant now fully making its way to all corners of Belmont Park, his attack on any horse who didn't run in the previous two Triple Crown races of course included the winner Tonalist who missed the Derby due to his failure to accrue enough career earnings to make the top 20 cut. For Tonalist's owner Robert Evans, the issue threatened to overshadow his biggest victory as an owner. Deciding not to get caught up in the Coburn rant, Evans politely but tersely responded with a "I have no comment." to NBC's Bob Costas looking to get his thoughts on the matter. What Evans did discuss when it came to Coburn however was his understanding of how much of a disappointment it was for his counterpart to deal with such a rough loss on the doorstep to the Triple Crown. Evans saw it firsthand when Pleasant Colony failed to win the Belmont Stakes to become 12th Triple Crown winner in 1981 since the colt was owned by his father Thomas. "This is very satisfying. Yesterday, I went to my father's grave and thanked him for putting me in the position to be doing this. And I came in 1981 to the Belmont, when we had high hopes for Pleasant Colony. I've been where Steve Coburn's been and it's not fun when you don't win."

Joining Evans in the winner's circle was Tonalist's trainer Christophe Clement who prior to his victory in the Belmont Stakes, had done most of his winning on the turf. Just like his owner, Clement was unapologetic for spoiling the California Chrome party. "There's nothing negative. California Chrome created a wonderful thing. Five-thirty in the morning, 500 or 600 people came to see him train. That was great. It was wonderful to see the large crowds. But it's nothing negative. I'm sure we will manage to find a way to sleep tonight."
Last but not least, those looking for a quote out of Art Sherman instead were directed to meet with his son Alan about 20 minutes after the race. Acknowledging the extreme disappointment his father was going through at the moment, Alan was left to field the questions about what happened. "I saw Victor starting to squeeze on him a little and he didn't respond the way he has in the past."

It wasn't until much later in the evening when the apocalyptic rush to get home from the track was already becoming a separate news item around Elmont, that Art Sherman shared some thoughts on the race. It was also during that time when Sports Illustrated's Tim Layden tweeted out that California Chrome had suffered an injury leaving the gate which would account for the bobble that was seen in his first few strides. "Trainer Art Sherman just said California Chrome may have injured himself leaving the gate. Kicked rt (right) front leg with rt (right) rear." Admitting that there was in fact an injury, Sherman allowed the argument that it may have had a negative impact on California Chrome's performance. "It's like having a fingernail pulled out. I've got a feeling it did."

While the injury was now becoming a story that would take clearer shape the next day, the fact of the matter was that California Chrome had only achieved the distinction of being the 13th Triple Crown failure at the Belmont Stakes since Affirmed last completed the feat back in 1978. The next day figured to be filled with anti-Steve Coburn rants, given the already fierce backlash seen on social media. It also would be filled with yet more arguments that the Triple Crown series should finally be changed. Either way, California Chrome was in that undesirable realm where his impressive wins in the Kentucky Derby and the Preakness were being overshadowed with his failure in the Belmont Stakes. The failure to attain immortality was so close but yet so far away. Again.

THE DAY AFTER

Not even 24 hours later, Steve Coburn was still boiling hot. Even after having a night to clear his head and rethink his comments said in the heat of the moment right after California Chrome went down in defeat on the doorstep to the Triple Crown, Coburn didn't let up one bit when it came to the points he made a day earlier.

Sensing an opportunity to build on his much-publicized words, Good Morning America and ESPN both jumped at the chance to give Coburn another platform to rant. Instead of making a seemingly bad situation better for himself, Coburn poured more gasoline on the verbal fire with an analogy that was cringe-worthy. During the Good Morning America segment, Coburn again repeated his assertion that it was unfair for horses who skipped the Derby or Preakness be allowed to run in the Belmont by saying it would be "like me, whose 6-2, playing basketball against a kid in a wheelchair." Taken aback by the quote, the Good Morning America crew followed up by asking if he thought that what he had just said was offensive to some. Coburn however was unbowed. "No. I'm jury trying to compare the two. Is it fair for me to play against a child in a wheelchair? Is it fair for them to hold their horses back?" Clearly there was no turning back now for Coburn and his all-out assault on the state of horse racing.

Meanwhile back at the Belmont barn before Coburn's interviews with Good Morning America and ESPN, Art Sherman emerged to meet with the media after refusing to take questions the day prior, so deep was his shock over California Chrome's defeat. Naturally the first question regarded his boss' comments to NBC which Sherman did his best to distance himself from while also not burning any bridges to California Chrome's ownership. "I think in the heat of the moment, he got a little angry. He hasn't been in the game long and he hadn't had any bad luck. The horses aren't cowards, the people aren't cowards. He'll probably make a pretty good apology for that."

Talk finally got back to California Chrome himself and Sherman confirmed the late Saturday evening report that his colt had indeed gotten injured coming out of the starting gate in the Belmont. Replays would show that Matterhorn, who was in the third post right next to California Chrome, had stepped on his right front foot as they broke from the gate. A cut opened up on California Chrome's right front tendon but the wound was considered superficial and not career-threatening by any means according to Sherman. Asked however if the cut prevented California Chrome from winning the Triple Crown, Sherman noted that "It couldn't have helped him any. It might have been stinging him and he might not have been comfortable. I watched him the last 70 yards and he didn't have his usual kick. It was scary to come back to the barn and see his foot bleeding. Other than having about a quarter of his hoof being taken off, it's OK. It should heal in about three weeks and then he'll get some needed time off. The Triple Crown is a rough trail. We'll fight another day."

California Chrome was seen later on in the day Sunday with a white wrap around his foot but Sherman reiterated that he would race again one day, with the Breeders' Cup Classic likely being his next target to shoot for as far as his return to action. Reflecting on everything he had just gone through in the last five weeks, Sherman vowed he wouldn't lose his perspective. "You can't be a hero all the time. I did win the Kentucky Derby and the Preakness, and the horse has made more than $3 million. I think I'll get a pretty good reception when I go back to Los Alamitos."

Finally Sherman was asked his thoughts on whether there would be another Triple Crown winner after California Chrome became the latest failure to achieve the feat. "Not unless there are changes made and the races are spaced further apart. I don't think so, unless you get a really freaky horse." Honest and to the point, Sherman joined the growing chorus of critics of the current Triple Crown setup. Somewhere Wayne Lukas was nodding.

THE APOLOGY

Hindsight as they say is always 20/20. Even when it comes a few days late as was the case with the mea culpa offered up by Steve Coburn 48 hours after one of the all-time rants became the talk of the sporting world. Sensing the extreme negativity his words generated for all involved, Coburn went right back on Good Morning American early on the Monday after the Belmont Stakes. With tears percolating in his eyes, Coburn admitted that he was "very ashamed of myself, very ashamed. I need to apologize to a lot of people because I was wrong." Coburn was joined for the second Good Morning America interview with wife Carol who of course gained unwanted fame after she failed to calm her husband down right after the race, instead earning a sharp rebuke in the process. Carol would get a public apology from her husband during the interview, along with Tonalis't owner and trainer Robert Evans and Christophe Clement respectively. "Tonalist ran a beautiful race and they deserved that. I didn't meant to take anything away from them."

Putting the finishing touches to his public comeuppance and perhaps wrapping up the entire California Chrome journey over the last five weeks, Coburn went to the heart of his emotions after the disappointment of the Belmont. "This is American's horse and I wanted so much for him to win the Triple Crown for the people of America, and I was very emotional. It's part of a learning process. I'm going to do better."

EPILOGUE

It wasn't meant to be. The same narrative that was spoken after the Triple Crown failures of Real Quiet and Silver Charm. Of Funny Cide and Smarty Jones. Of Big Brown and now California Chrome. The drought officially reached 37 years and counting once Tonalist crossed the Belmont Stakes wire in first, with a tiring California Chrome finishing in a dead heat for fourth. The heartache and disappointment was palpable at Belmont Park once the result became official and California Chrome became the 13th horse since Affirmed last won the Triple Crown to fail in the Belmont after winning the first two legs. Outside of Steve Coburn's rant to end all rants, talk once again would come from all corners about whether or not there could ever be another Triple Crown winner. Whether the Triple Crown series did in fact needed to be changed to reflect the current state of horse racing.

But maybe it simply was not California Chrome's time. Maybe the racing gods didn't find California Chrome worthy of joining the immortal club of 11 Triple Crown winners. Maybe California Chrome getting stepped on by Matterhorn coming out of the gate was the racing gods making sure the Triple Crown would have to wait for at least another year.. Just like Spectacular Bid stepping on the pin prior to the Belmont when he looked like a can't miss. Just like the monsoon-like rains that turned Big Sandy into a quagmire, greatly impeding Funny Cide's inside post along the rail where the mud was at its deepest in his failed Triple Crown attempt. Just like War Emblem stumbling right out of the gate under Victor Espinoza, finishing his chances before he even got started. All of these developments were tough to stomach, so close were these terrific horses from reaching the pinnacle of their sport. However in the end as they say, it simply was not their time.

Despite yet another massive letdown after California Chrome failed to win the Triple Crown, the fact of the matter is that come the first Saturday in May next spring, the journey begins again for another 20 horses in their quest for racing's hallowed ground. All of the talk of changing the format or spacing out the races will all go away as the public collectively returns to Churchill Downs either in person or through television. Hoping maybe this is the year. This is the year where the next monster horse begins his run to the elusive Triple Crown. And maybe; just maybe this same superstar horse will complete the journey in crossing the finish line first in the Derby, Preakness, and than finally the Belmont Stakes.

Part of the allure of the Triple Crown series is the thrill of the chase. While the chase has gone on longer than maybe anticipated, the payoff figures to be that much sweeter when it finally does happen again. Immortality was never meant to be easy as the now growing list of 13 close call horses and their connections could tell you. However maybe somewhere a foal is being born right at this moment. He comes out of his mother's womb with an excitable kick. He quickly stand up on his own and within weeks is running like the wind. He begins to get acquainted with a racetrack, pushed along by the right combination of trainer, exercise rider, and owner. He grows more and more powerful by the day. He begins to burn around the track with a confident and easy stride that raises eyebrows. He rumbles through a 2-year-old campaign that brings hype for the next season's Triple Crown series. He smashes the competition in either the Wood Memorial, the Santa Anita Derby, or the Florida Derby. He goes into the Kentucky Derby as the "now" horse and comes through with a monster finishing kick in drawing away from the field. He goes on to dominate the Preakness, with nary a sign of effort in disposing of his foes. He goes into the Belmont Stakes with the entire nation behind him, basking in the glow of the media attention and hype. He gets a clean release out of the Belmont Park gates, rampaging through the first half-mile. He moves around the far turn with the same powerful kick that he showed in all of his previous runway victories. He straightens out for the homestretch, in front of the pack as the wire moves closer. And closer. And closer. And

than..

....

THE IMMORTAL FRATERNITY

It had been 36 years since Affirmed beat Alydar for the third straight time to become the 11th Triple Crown winner in the over 100-year history of horse racing. The streak would of course reach 37 after California Chrome came up just short in the Belmont Stakes after winning both the Kentucky Derby and the Preakness. California Chrome's defeat would in turn further immortalize those 11 previous Triple Crown champions who feat becomes all the more impressive as the drought goes on.

1. Sir Barton (1919): The charter member of the Triple Crown club, Sir Barton was foaled in Lexington, Kentucky and purchased for a pricey at that time $10,000. No one would have possibly foreseen what was to come as Sir Barton fell on his face as a two-year-old, losing all six races he was entered in. In fact Sir Barton was only entered into the Kentucky Derby as a means to set up a stablemate for a late run. However Sir Barton went with his own plan, showcasing a driven speed he had failed to produce just a year earlier. With jockey John Loftus aboard, Sir Barton swept the Triple Crown series and finished his career with 13 wins and a total of $116,857 in earnings.

2. Gallant Fox (1930): Like with Sir Barton before him, Gallant Fox was not an overly impressive 2-year-old colt as he won only 2 of his first 7 races. However in following the path of Sir Barton, Gallant Fox exploded under jockey Earl Sande to win the Triple Crown in 1930 as part of a 9 wins in 10 race stretch. Not wanting to risk injury, while also having a desire to cash in while Gallant Fox was at his highest stud value, owner Belair Stud retired his champion after his 3-year-old campaign. Overall Gallant Fox was victorious in a dominant 11 of 17 starts and earned a total of $328,165 in earnings. In addition, Gallant Fox went down in history as being the only Triple Crown champ to sire another, this in the form of future star Omaha.

3. Omaha (1935): The son of Gallant Fox certainly had the genes to succeed but he also had a lot to live up to as the offspring of a dominant champion. Omaha quickly showed he was up to the task. Once again Belair Stud had a star on his hands and jockey Willie Sanders rode Omaha flawlessly through all three Triple Crown conquests. Omaha would finish his career with 9 wins in 22 starts, earning a total of $154,755.

4. War Admiral (1937): The Triple Crown was becoming something of habit, with three champions in seven years by the time War Admiral completed the trifecta. War Admiral was interesting in that he was the son of all-time great Man O'War but his smallish size left many openly wondering where his father's genes were. However there was no debating War Admiral's heart and determination to enter the winner's circle as he went a perfect 8-for-8 in his three-year old campaign which of course include the Triple Crown sweep under jockey Charles Kurtsinge and owner George Conway.

War Admiral's dominance extended well beyond his three-year-old campaign as he would finish with 21 wins in 26 career races. Outside of his Triple Crown victories, perhaps War Admiral is best known for a match race defeat he suffered at the hands of Seabiscuit which was brought back to the public's consciousness with the Disney big picture adaptation of his rival. Overall War Admiral finished with career earnings of $273,240.

5. Whirlaway (1941): The fourth horse to take the Triple Crown in 11 years was "Mr. Longtail" Whirlaway. Given the nickname due to his extra-long flowing tail, Whirlaway was the first major score for owner Warren Wright who was trying to put his Calumet Farm into the mainstream racing community. Unlike the champions that came before him, Whirlaway was a difficult horse to control at times due to his propensity to run wide which went against the number 1 racing sacrament to save as much ground as possible. Hall of Fame jockey Eddie Arcaro was enlisted to break Whirlaway from this habit and with Wright's blessing, decided that the use of blinkers would keep his colt focused. The strategy was a smashing success as Whirlaway was a 'Runaway' winner in the Kentucky Derby, setting a record time of 2:01 2/5 in his eight-length victory which stood for 20 years. One of the most active horses of his time, Whirlaway would win 32 races out of 60 career starts which helped him pass the half-a-million dollar mark in career earnings with $561,161.

6. Count Fleet (1943): Count Fleet was assigned a record 132 pounds for his winning Kentucky Derby which he won going away in his short but impressive career. Overall Count Fleet would win all six of his career races which came as a three-year-old under jockey Johnny Logden. Owner John Hertz cut short Count Fleet's career in order not to risk his stud future and the riches that came with it.

7. Assault (1946): As hard as it is to imagine today, Assault's Triple Crown victory was the seventh in 16 years which led to some talk in the industry about making the series more difficult. As far as Assault was concerned, he was one of only two Texas-breeds to win the Kentucky Derby. What makes all of Assault's accomplishments even more impressive was the fact that he became a champion despite suffering an early foreleg injury that left the extremity crooked. The son of Bold Ventura would reach the winner's circle twice as a two-year-old for owner Robert Kleberg and trainer Max Hirsch and Assault would turn it up another notch as a three-year-old in winning 8 of his 15 starts. Unlike most of the other Triple Crown champions, Assault continued to race for a few years after his feat, winning his last race at the age of 7. Overall Assault would claim victory in 18 of his 42 races for a career earnings haul of $675,470.

8. Citation (1950): Widely considered the best racehorse of the century along with Man O'War, Citation gave Calumet Farms and trainer Ben Jones a second Triple Crown winner in seven years. Virtually unbeatable, Citation was stunning in his success as he won a ridiculous 27-of-29 starts in his two-and three-year-old campaigns. Even more staggering was a 16-race winning streak that Citation accumulated at one point.

9. Secretariat (1973): Along similar lines of California Chrome ending a long Triple Crown drought. the legendary Secretariat became the first colt to join the immortality fraternity in 23 years. Not only did Secretariat set a Kentucky Derby record in coming under the wire first in 1:59 2/5 (which would be the first sub-2:00 minute Derby time ever, since broken by Monarchos in 2001) but he also engineered what is widely considered the greatest racing performance in history at the Belmont Stakes a few weeks later. It was at Belmont where Secretariat claimed victory by a staggering 31 lengths in what anyone who witnessed it would describe as the most awesome race ever seen. Just like with Seabiscuit, Secretariat got his own motion picture produced about his incredible racing life.

10. Seattle Slew (1977): Went into the Kentucky Derby undefeated in six races which earned him 1-2 odds. Might have had the worst start ever for a Derby champ as Seattle Slew almost fell face first coming out of the gate which instantly put him behind the early leaders by 6-and-a-half lengths. Jockey Jean Cruguet didn't panic however as Seattle Slew eventually picked off his foes one-by-one until winning it all by a 1 3/4 length margin. Slew would tempt fate again as a four-year-old in almost succumbing to illness but he eventually got back onto the track where he defeated fellow Triple Crown champ Affirmed in the Marlboro Cup. He would retire with 14 wins in 17 races for a total earnings of $1,208,726.

11. Affirmed (1978): Many believed Affirmed would be the last ever Triple Crown champion as the drought to California Chrome stretched to over 30 years. Ridden by Steve Cauthen, Affirmed's often-vanquished prime foe Alydar also became just as famous due to their ongoing rivalry. After Affirmed beat Alydar four of the six times they met as two-year-olds, they became the prime contenders for the Triple Crown series. Affirmed won all three duels in the classics and 7-of-10 lifetime meetings overall. He would retire with 22 wins in 26 career races while earning more than $2 million.

THE CLOSE CALLS

No one ever said it was going to be easy. With thoroughbred horses no longer running as often as they did even as recently as the 1970's and with their fragility seemingly as delicate as ever, plenty of arguments have been made that the Triple Crown in its current state is nothing but a pipe dream for all. Fueling this talk of course is the unending Triple Crown drought that stretched all the way back to Affirmed in 1978. Further adding doubt to the possibility of such a feat being accomplished again were the 12 horses prior to California Chrome who won the Kentucky Derby-Preakness double but who than failed to close the deal in the Belmont Stakes. From Spectacular Bid in 1979 to I'll Have Another in 2012, all 12 failed for varying and sometimes unbelievable reasons which added to the mystique and frustration of the Triple Crown chase.

1. Spectacular Bid (1979): Spectacular Bid aimed to become the third Triple Crown winner in a row after Seattle Slew in 1977 and Affirmed in 1978. After winning the Kentucky Derby and the Preakness with little difficulty, Bid seemed a lock to take the Belmont Stakes and the title of 12th Triple Crown champion. However in the first indication of the racing gods wanting to alter the storybook ending, Spectacular Bid reportedly stepped on a safety pin the day before the Belmont Stakes which left his stride negatively impacted for the race. Spectacular Bid would finish third that day as the 1-5 favorite, with many blaming the pin as the reason for his defeat. Little did anyone know how long it would be before another Triple Crown champion would appear.

2. Pleasant Colony (1981): Pleasant Colony was a freakishly tall horse who had a loopy stride that made him seem like a very unlikely Triple Crown contender. However Pleasant Colony took home both the Derby and Preakness after finishing a dull fifth in the Florida Derby. Despite all the forward momentum Pleasant Colony had, he would finish third in the Belmont behind Summing by 1 1/2 lengths.

3. Alysheba (1987): Alysheba defied many odds along the way to winning the Derby and the Preakness. Months before the Derby Alysheba was crossed off most contender lists after having to undergo surgery to fix a breathing problem. Alysheba got the last laugh however, taking home the roses despite stumbling down the stretch on his way to victory. The momentum died in the Belmont however as Alysheba was checked sharply going around the far turn, ruining his stride and resulting in a 14-length defeat to Bet Twice.

4. Sunday Silence (1989): Along the same lines of the rivalry between Affirmed and Alydar, Sunday Silence and Easy Goer's epic duels in 1989 served as the story of the racing year. Easy Goer went into the Derby as the clear favorite but he would be upset by Sunday Silence both in Louisville and again two weeks later in the Preakness. Easy Goer would get the last laugh however, denying Sunday Silence the Triple Crown with an eight-length win in the Belmont.

5. Silver Charm (1997): Bob Baffert announced his arrival as a top notch trainer with a monster horse by the name of Silver Charm. Highly touted for the entire prep season, Silver Charm looked like a sure bet to end the Triple Crown drought which had reached 19 years. It appeared all those predictions of greatness would come true as Silver Charm led the Belmont down the stretch but was overtaken by Touch Gold in the final furlong to lose by less than a length.

6. Real Quiet (1998): Just one year after Silver Charm came oh-so-close to earning the Triple Crown, Baffert came right back with maybe an even stronger contender in Real Quiet. Once again Baffert saw his horse lead down the stretch of the Belmont, this time by an even bigger four-length margin with less than a quarter of a mile to go. Unbelievably, Victory Gallup came charging out of nowhere in a mad dash to the finish line, edging out Real Quiet by literally a nose. No Triple Crown close call would be more heartbreaking.

7. Charismatic (1999): For the third year in a row, a Triple Crown threat was denied but this time it was trainer D. Wayne Lukas and not Bob Baffert who suffered the rough defeat. Unlike Real Quiet and Silver Charm the two previous years, Charismatic was ignored going into the Derby as he went off at 31-1 odds. However his momentum built to a crescendo in the Belmont Stakes where

Charismatic, under the ride of Chris Antley, took a brief lead at the far turn before giving way to spoiler Lemon Drop Kid. Tragically, Charismatic broke two bones in his left during his third place finish. Images of a crying Antley as he tried in vain to hold Charismatic's leg in order to prevent him from putting any weight on it, became an unforgettable reminder of the risk thoroughbred horses undertake in racing. Fortunately Charismatic recovered and to this day stands stud.

8. War Emblem (2002): Once again it was Bob Baffert who took a third swing at the elusive Triple Crown but this time it was behind a front-running surprise in the temperamental War Emblem. Unfortunately fate got in the way again as War Emblem stumbled badly at the start of the Belmont Stakes, nearly putting his nose to the ground. To make matters worse, War Emblem was also immediately bumped by Magic Weisner, putting him rank for half the race. True to his ability, War Emblem rallied to take a brief lead on the backstretch but than faded all the way to eighth which was the furthest ever a Triple Crown attempting horse would ever finish.

9. Funny Cide (2003): This popular gelding was an instant hit publicly as Funny Cide was owned by a group of childhood friends who barely ponied up enough money to claim him. The late Bobby Frankel's Empire Maker was seen as a monster horse going into the Derby capable of winning the crown. However Funny Cide knocked off Empire Maker in shocking fashion and than dominated the

Preakness in winning by eight lengths. However a rested Empire Maker (who skipped the Preakness) returned the favor to Funny Cide in the Belmont, ending yet another potential Triple Crown dreamer.

10. Smarty Jones (2004): Out of the 12 "Dozen Denied" Triple Crown horses since Affirmed last won it all in 1978, Smarty Jones was considered the biggest upset as far as his failure to bring it home in the Belmont. Despite being ridden by a relatively unknown jockey in Stewart Elliott, Smarty Jones dominated the Kentucky Derby and Preakness which added to his undefeated record. The aura of invincibility was through the roof for Smarty Jones going to the Belmont but two big factors conspired to deny him the crown. The first issue were reports that the rest of the jockeys in the field worked together to prevent Smarty Jones from winning by trying to collectively box him in at the rail, thus making him work hard to break free. The second and perhaps bigger problem was Elliott making the stretch run with Smarty Jones a furlong too early according to multiple experts who witnessed the race firsthand. Elliott showed his big stage inexperience with his premature move and as a result, despite Smarty Jones taking the lead early in the stretch, Birdstone was able to rally late to catch him. So devastating was the defeat that Birdstone's trainer Nick Zito felt the need to apologized for derailing the bid afterwards.

11. Big Brown (2008): Like Smarty Jones before him, Big Brown entered the Belmont Stakes undefeated after winning the Derby handily and than setting a record-time in smashing the Preakness. Controversy followed Big Brown due to the outspoken nature and checkered past of his trainer Rick Dutrow. After Dutrow guaranteed a Triple Crown, Big Brown shockingly pulled up on his run halfway through the race as jockey Kent Desormeaux moved him to the side of the track to an eventual complete stop. Big Brown would fail to even finish the race. While no one knew exactly what went wrong, the brutally hot weather (race-time temperature was 100 degrees) reignited talk that the racing gods just didn't want Big Brown to join the immortality club.

12. I'll Have Another (2012): Similar to Big Brown four years earlier, I'll Have Another was prepped by a controversial trainer in Doug O'Neill who was fresh off a suspension due to one of his horses testing positive for a banned substance. After surprisingly winning the Kentucky Derby with a late run, I'll Have Another doubled up with a nice Preakness score which elevated the hype machine for a public that had now waited 34 years since the last Triple Crown champion. Just a day before the Belmont Stakes however, I'll Have Another was scratched as O'Neill cited a vague leg injury. Rumors circulated that I'll Have Another was being targeted by the New York Racing Association for drug testing which O'Neill denied. The whole issue remains a mystery to this day.

ABOUT THE AUTHOR

Michael Keneski is a freelance sports writer whose works include "Hockey Fights Of Yesteryear 1 & 2" and "The Super Season: The Story of The New York Giants' Super Bowl 45 Team." He lives in Long Island, New York with his wife Allison and two children Ryan and Emma.